Particulars of dry docks, wet docks, wharves, &c., on the Thames ..

Charles H Jordan

PARTICULARS

OF

DRY DOCKS, WET DOCKS, WHARVES, &c.,

ON THE THAMES.

COMPILED BY

CHAS. H. JORDAN. M.I.N.A.,

HONORARY FREEMAN OF THE WORSHIPFUL COMPANY OF SHIPWRIGHTS,
AUTHOR OF 'TABULATED WEIGHTS OF IRON AND STEEL' PRINCIPAL SURVEYOR
ON THE CHIEF SHIP SURVEYORS STAFF OF
LLOYD'S REGISTER OF BRITISH AND FOREIGN SHIPPING.

———•◦•———

SECOND EDITION, REVISED AND ENLARGED

———•◦•———

LONDON
E. & F. N. SPON, LTD., 125, STRAND.

NEW YORK
SPON & CHAMBERLAIN, 12, CORTLANDT STREET
1904.

LONDON
PRINTED AT THE PRINTING HOUSE OF
LLOYD'S REGISTER OF BRITISH AND FOREIGN SHIPPING,
64, SOUTHWARK STREET, S E

PREFACE TO THE SECOND EDITION

———.o———

The favourable reception accorded by the Shipping public to the first edition of 'Particulars of Dry Docks, &c, on the Thames,' has induced the Compiler to prepare the present edition

The new work will be found to contain much additional information, viz —Particulars of the *Wet* Docks, a list of all the Wharves and River side premises on both sides of the Thames, from London Bridge to Blackwall, a list of Lines of Vessels and the Docks used by them on the Thames and a list of the Public Mooring Buoys in the River, besides Maps and other information.

A complete index has also been added in order to make the contents of the work, as far as possible, available for instant use

The additional information will, it is anticipated, enhance the value of this little work in the eyes of those whose business necessitates an acquaintance with the Docks, &c, on the Thames

CHAS H JORDAN.

LONDON, *July*, 1904.

a 2

(IV)

PREFACE TO THE FIRST EDITION

————— o —————

On taking up my duties as surveyor in London some eleven years since, it occurred to me that a list of the Dry Docks on the Thames, with particulars as to their whereabouts and the best means of getting to them, would be very useful to me. I therefore availed myself of opportunities to collect this information, to which I added from time to time particulars as to the dimensions of the docks. After a few years the list became so useful that I was led to the idea of publishing it for the benefit of others, who like myself were interested in the Dry Docks on the Thames.

I have endeavoured to obtain the dimensions of the Docks as accurately as possible particularly as regards the depth of sill below T H W. This has necessitated a considerable amount of trouble, which however has been very much lessened by the kind assistance which I have received from the Proprietors of the Docks.

CHAS H JORDAN,

LONDON, *July* 1882,

(v)

CONTENTS.

NAME OF DOCK.	Length.		Breadth at entrance.		Sill.			Constant for height of high water.*	Material of			Closed by
	Extreme.	On bottom.	Top.	Bottom	Relation to dock bottom.	Depth below T.H.W.			Bottom.	Sides.	Head.	
	ft. in.	ft. in.	ft. in.	ft. in.	ft. in.	ft. in.		ft. in.				
BLACKWALL POINT . .	475 0	472 0	60 0	52 0	..	Level.	21 0	+ 0 4	Wood on concrete.	Wood	.. Wood	.. Iron caisson..
BRITANNIA	300 0	293 0	47 0	40 0	1 6 above.		15 6	— 5 2	Wood	.. Brick and wood.	Brick	.. Wood caisson
CANAL . . . . . Large	295 0	294 0	61 0	61 0	0 10 above.		17 6	— 5 2	Wood	.. Wood	.. Brick	.. Wood gates..
CANAL . . . . . Small	258 0	256 0	49 0	49 0	1 8 above.		16 0	— 4 8	Wood	.. Wood	.. Wood	.. Wood gates..
CUBITT TOWN	382 0	369 0	49 0	44 9	4 6 above.		18 0	— 2 8	Concrete .	Wood on concrete.	Brick	.. Wood gates ..
DEPTFORD GREEN..	417 0	410 0	65 0	51 0	..	Level.	20 4	— 0 4	Wood on concrete.	Wood	.. Wood	.. Iron caisson..
EAST INDIA.	290 0	286 0	55 0	52 0	..	Level.	17 0	— 3 8	Wood	.. Wood	.. Brick	.. Iron caisson..
FOUNTAIN	154 0	151 6	47 6	34 9	..	Level.	14 4	— 6 4	Wood	.. Wood	.. Brick	.. Wood caisson
GLENGALL	345 0	339 0	42 0	42 0	..	Level.	16 3	— 4 5	Wood	.. Brick	.. Wood	.. Wood gates..
GREEN'S . . . . . Large	472 0	471 0	65 0	65 0	1 6 above.		23 0	+ 2 4	Granite on concrete.	Granite on concrete.	Brick and granite.	.. Iron caisson..
GREEN'S . . . . . Small	335 0	333 0	62 0	51 0	..	Level.	17 6	— 3 2	Wood	.. Brick	.. Brick	.. Iron caisson..
HORSEFERRY	225 0	225 0	42 0	42 0	..	Level.	16 9	— 3 11	Wood	.. Wood	.. Brick	.. Iron caisson..
METROPOLITAN . . .	325 0	329 0	49 0	36 6	0 4½ above.		14 0	— 6 8	Wood	.. Wood	.. Wood	.. Iron caisson..
MILLWALL	450 0	430 0	65 0	65 0	2 0 above.		25 0	+ 4 4½	Brick and masonry.	Brick and masonry.	Brick and masonry.	.. Iron caisson..

* The heights of High Water on the sill may be ascertained for any day in the year, by applying (according to the sign) the annexed constant in this

Where situated.		Proprietors, City Office, Telegraphic Address, and Telephone Number.	How reached from the City.
Locality.	Side of River.		
st Greenwich, S.E.	South	John Stewart & Son, Ltd., 22, Billiter Street, E.C. "Steamships, London." "1128 Avenue."	Train from Fenchurch St. to Poplar, and 'bus through the Blackwall Tunnel.
illwall, E.	North	W. C. Reeder & Co., 1, Railway Place, Fenchurch Street, E.C.	Train from Fenchurch St. to W. I. Dock, and 'bus to Millwall.
oplar, E.	North	John Stewart & Son, Ltd., 22, Billiter Street, E.C. "Steamships, London." "4428 Avenue."	Train from Fenchurch St. to South Dock.
oplar, E.	North		
abitt Town, E.	North	Rait & Gardner, 155, Fenchurch Street, E.C. "Repairs, London." "4091 Avenue."	Train from Fenchurch St. to North Greenwich.
eptford Green, S.E.	South	Deptford Dry Dock Co., Ltd., 88, Bishopsgate Street Within, E.C. "Shoring, London." "71 Deptford."	Train from Cannon St. to Deptford.
, Orchard Place, Blackwall, E.	North	London Graving Dock Co., Ltd., 114, Fenchurch Street, E.C. "Augmented, London." "5601 Avenue."	Train from Fenchurch St. to Blackwall.
ermondsey, S.E.	South	Mills & Knight, 155, Fenchurch Street, E.C. "4182 Avenue." "553 Hop."	Train to Spa Road (S. E. & C. R.), or 'bus to St. James's Church
illwall, E.	North	Glengall Iron Works, Ltd. "Glengall, London"	Train from Fenchurch St. to W. I. Dock, and 'bus to Millwall.
ackwall, E.	North	R. & H. Green, Ltd., 13, Fenchurch Avenue, E.C. "Green, Blackwall, London." "203 Eastern."	Train from Fenchurch St. to Poplar.
ackwall, E.	North		
5,Rotherhithe Street, S.E.	South	J. McDowall & Co. "Dowall, London." "808 Hop."	Train from Fenchurch St. to Stepney, and boat across River.
eptford Green, S.E.	South	Deptford Dry Docks Co., Ltd., 88, Bishopsgate street Within, E.C. "Shoring, London." "71 Deptford."	Train from Cannon St. to Deptford.
illwall Docks, E.	North	Rait & Gardiner, 155, Fenchurch Street, E.C. "Repairs, London." "4091 Avenue."	Train from Fenchurch St. to Millwall Dock.

NOTE.—Trinity Datum (Trinity H. W. Mark), or mean level of High Water Ordinary Springs, is 20 ft. 8 ins. above the Admiralty Datum, or mean level of Low Water Ordinary Springs, and 12 ft. 8 ins. above the Ordnance Datum.

Spring Rise or Spring Range { or mean level of High Water Ordinary Springs above mean level of Low Water Ordinary Springs = 20 ft. 8 ins.
Neap Rise or mean level of High Water Ordinary Neaps above mean level of Low Water Ordinary Springs = 17 ft. 3 ins. } At the Shadwell upper entrance
Neap Range or mean level of High Water Ordinary Neaps above mean level of Low Water Ordinary Neaps = 13 ft. 1 in. of the London Docks.

Spring tides are those which occur at, or soon after, new moon and full moon. Neap tides are those which occur at, or soon after, the completion of the moon's first and third quarter of lunation.

NAME OF DOCK.	Length.		Breadth at surface.		Sill.		Depth below T.H.W.	Constant for height of high water †		Material of			Closed by
	Extreme.	On bottom.	Top.	Between dock bottom.	Relation to dock bottom.					Bottom.	Sides.	Head.	
	ft. in.	ft. in.	ft. in.	ft. in.	ft. in.		ft. in.	ft. in.					
NELSON	370 0	370 0	68 0	68 0	1 0 above.		20 1	— 9	7	Wood and concrete.	Wood and concrete and wood.	Concrete	Iron caisson..
POPLAR	390 0	373 0	52 0	5 0	1 3 above.		15 0	— 1	4	Wood on concrete.	Wood and brick.	Brick	Wood gates..
PRINCES	255 0	230 0	44 0	41 0	1 0 above.		15 5	— 4	11	Wood on concrete.	Wood	Brick	Wood gates ..
REGENT	281 6	277 0	30 0	18 0	0 6 above.		18 7	— 2	1	Wood	Wood	Brick	Wood caisson
ROYAL ALBERT . LARGE	521 0	500 0	68 0	59 0	3 0 above.		22 3	+ 1	7§	Concrete	Concrete	Concrete	Iron caisson..
ROYAL ALBERT . SMALL	425 0	408 2+	68 0	59 0	3 0 above.		22 3	+ 1	7§	Concrete	Concrete	Concrete	Iron caisson..
THAMES . . . . . LARGE	475 0	472 0+	65 0	56 0	2 9 above.		21 0	+ 3	4	Brick and masonry.	Brick and masonry.	Brick and masonry.	Iron caisson..
THAMES . . . . . SMALL	355 0	335 0+	46 0	41 0	2 0 above.		21 0	+ 0	4	Brick and masonry.	Brick and masonry.	Brick and masonry.	Iron caisson..
TILBURY . . . . . No. 1	842 3	825 3	78 0	69 0	.. Level.		35 0	+14	4	Wood on concrete.	Brick and masonry.	Caisson	Iron caissons ..
TILBURY . . . . . No. 2	841 3	825 3	67 0	60 0	.. Level.		30 0	+ 9	4	Wood on concrete.	Brick and masonry.	Caisson	Iron caissons ..
UNION . . . . . . UPPER	381 0	328 0	46 6	45 5	1 1½ above.		17 4	— 3	4	Wood on concrete.	Brick and concrete.	Brick	Wood gates ..
UNION . . . . . . MIDDLE	252 0	250 0	44 2	38 8	1 2½ above.		15 10	— 4	11	Wood	Brick, concrete, wood	Brick	Iron caisson..
UNION . . . . . . LOWER	613 0	610 0	60 0	51 0	2 0 above.		20 6	— 0	2	Concrete	Concrete	Concrete	Iron gates ..
WEST INDIA	153 0	143 0	64 0	52 0	0 0 above.		25 0	+ 2	4§	Concrete and wood	Brick and masonry.	Brick	Iron caisson..

* See footnote on page 6.
† Arson included.
§ These docks are situated inside wet docks, and are therefore not much affected by the fall of the tide, and the depth of water on the sill may be

Where situated.		Proprietors, City Office, Telegraphic Address, and Telephone Number.	How reached from the City.
Locality.	Side of River.		
otherhithe, S.E...	..South	Mills & Knight, 155, Fenchurch Street, E.C. "4482 Avenue." "22 Deptford."	Train from Fenchurch St. to Limehouse or W.I. Docks and boat across River, or train (Met. Rly.) to Rotherhithe.
ubitt Town, E...	..North	Brown's Dry Dock & Engineering Co., Ltd., 10, London Street, E.C. "Reparans, London" "2494 Avenue."	Train from Fenchurch St. to North Greenwich.
otherhithe Street, S.E.	South	Prince's Dry Dock Co., Ltd., 23, Billiter Street, E.C.	Train from Aldgate East to Rotherhithe, or from Fenchurch St. to stepney, and boat across River
lillwall, E. ..	..North	Glengall Iron Works, Ltd. "Glengall, London."	Train from Fenchurch St. to W. I. Dock, and 'bus to Millwall.
ilvertown, E. ..	..North	London & India Docks Co., 169, Leadenhall Street, E.C. "Dock, London." "4292 & 4296 Avenue."	Train from Fenchurch St. to Silvertown.
ilvertown, E. ..	..North		
Blackwall, E. ..	..North	Thames Iron Works, Ship Building & Engineering Co., Ltd., 17, Philpot Lane, E.C. "Accommodation, London." "583 Albert Dock." "Steamboats, London." "5959 Avenue."	Train from Fenchurch St. to Tidal Basin.
Blackwall, E. ..	..North		
Tilbury	..North	London & India Docks Co., 109, Leadenhall Street, E.C. "Dock, London." "4292 & 4296 Avenue."	Train from Fenchurch St. to Tilbury.
Tilbury	..North		
Bridge Road, Millwall, E.	North		
Bridge Road, Millwall, E.	North	Fletcher, Son & Fearnall, Ltd., 9, London Street, E.C. "Fletchers Docks, London." "109 Eastern."	Train from Fenchurch St. to West India Dock.
Bridge Road, Millwall, E.	North		
Poplar, E.	..North	London Graving Dock Co., Ltd., 114, Fenchurch Street, E.C. "Augmented, London." "5601 Avenue."	Train from Fenchurch to Poplar.

PARTICULARS OF GRIDIRONS

NAME.	Length.	Breadth.	Depth below T. H. W.	Constant for height of high water. *	Material.	Gross Tonnage of Vessel capable of being taken.	Where situated.	
							Locality.	Side of River.
	ft. in.	ft. in.	H. m.	H. m.		Tons.		
CROSSNESS GRIDIRON	290 0	43 0	11 6	— 3 2	Wood on piles	1100	Crossness	...south .
FOUNTAIN GRIDIRON	280 0	71 0	13 4	— 7 4	Wood on piles	2000	Bermondsey, S.E.	...south .
METROPOLITAN GRIDIRON .	193 0	38 0	11 0	— 6 8	Wood on piles	1300	Deptford, S.E. ..	...south .
NELSON PATENT SLIP . . .	215 0	29 6	15 7	— 5 4	Wood and iron	1000	Rotherhithe, S.E.	...South .
N. WOOLWICH GRIDIRON . .	160 0	60 0	6 6	—14 2	Wood on piles	500	N. Woolwich, S.E.	...North .
UNION GRIDIRON	127 0	43 0	14 9	— 5 11	Wood on piles	500	Bridge Rd., Millwall, E.	North .

* See footnote on page 6.

TIDE TABLE showing the difference of time,

		H. M.			H. M.			H. M.			H. M.
Aberdeen	.. sub. 1	50	Brighton	.. sub. 4	20	Dieppe	.. sub. 4	5	Glasgow (Port)	.. sub. 2	50
Aberystwith ..	.. add 4	55	Brill	.. add 0	50	Dover Pier ..	.. sub. 5	20	Gravesend ..	.. sub. 1	5
Aldborough ..	.. sub. 5	50	Bristol..	.. add 4	10	Dublin	.. sub. 5	0	Guernsey	.. add 3	25
Amsterdam ..	.. add 0	25	Calais	.. sub. 3	0	Dunbar	.. sub. 0	20	Hamburg	.. add 3	25
Antwerp	.. add 2	25	Cardiff	.. add 3	25	Dunkirk	.. sub. 2	30	Harwich	.. sub. 3	5
Archangel ..	.. add 3	25	Cardigan Bay ..	.. add 4	20	Edystone ..	.. add 2	40	Hastings	.. sub. 4	0
Baltimore ..	.. add 1	10	Cadiz	.. add 1	25	Exmouth Bar ..	.. add 3	40	Heligoland ..	.. sub. 5	55
Barnstaple Bar	.. sub. 2	55	Cherbourg ..	.. add 4	55	Falmouth ..	.. add 2	50	Helen St., St. ..	.. sub. 5	0
Beaumaris ..	.. sub. 4	20	Cork Harbour (Ent.)	add 1	55	Flushing	.. sub. 1	35	Harve de Grace	.. sub. 4	5
Berwick	.. sub. 0	20	Cowes	.. sub. 4	20	Fowey	.. add 2	55	Holyhead Bay..	.. sub. 4	35
Boulogne ..	.. sub. 4	0	Dartmouth ..	.. add 3	55	Gibraltar	.. sub. 2	55	Hull	.. add 3	30
Brest	.. add 1	55	Deal	.. sub. 3	20						

To find the time of High Water at any of the above ports, add or subtract

DIRECTIONS FOR ADJUSTING

Three sets of buoys are laid down at Greenhithe for the use of vessels requiring to swing for the adjustment of their the next high water at London Bridge. At spring tides it can

Proprietors, City Office, Telegraphic Address, and Telephone Number.	How reached from the City.
ondon County Council, Spring Gardens, S.W. "Witan, London." 3542.	Train from Cannon St. to Abbey Wood.
ills & Knight, 155, Fenchurch Street, E.C. "4482 Avenue." "553 Hop."	Train to Spa Road (S.E. & C. Rly.), or 'Bus to St. James's Church.
eneral Steam Navigation Co. "Generalship, London."	Train from Cannon St. to Deptford
ills & Knight, 155, Fenchurch Street, E.C. "4482 Avenue." "22 Deptford."	Train from Fenchurch St. to Limehouse or West India Docks, and Boat across River, or Train (Metropolitan Railway) to Rotherhithe or Deptford Rd.
ondon County Council, Spring Gardens, S.W. "Witan, London." 3542.	Train from Fenchurch St. to N. Woolwich.
letcher, Son & Fearnall, Ltd., 9, London Street, E.C. "199 Eastern."	Train from Fenchurch St. to West India Dock.

nearly, between London and other ports. By permission of Messrs. Smith & Ebbs.

	H.	M.				H.	M.				H.	M.				H.	M.
Humber (Ent.)	add 2	40	Needles		sub. 5	15	Ramsgate		sub. 3	15	Sunderland		add 0	25
Ipswich	sub. 2	35	Newcastle		add 1	25	Rochelle		add 1	10	Texel (Ent.)		add 1	10
Land's End	add 1	55	Nore Light		sub. 2	5	Rotterdam		add 0	55	Texel (Roads)		add 5	10
Leith Pier	sub. 0	15	Orfordness		sub. 3	45	Rouen		sub. 1	35	Tynemouth Bar		add 0	25
Limerick	add 2	45	Orkneys		sub. 4	5	Scarborough		add 1	50	Waterford Harbour	add 3	15
Lisbon	sub. 0	20	Ostend		sub. 2	15	Sheerness		sub. 2	35	Wells Harbour		add 3	25
Liverpool	sub. 3	35	Penzance		add 1	55	Shields		add 0	25	Whitby		add 1	10
Lynn Deeps	add 3	25	Plymouth		add 2	55	Southampton		sub. 2	55	Whitehaven		sub. 3	20
Margate Roads	sub. 2	50	Poole		sub. 5	35	Southwold		sub. 3	35	Wisbeach		add 4	55
Milford Haven	add 3	25	Portsmouth H'rbour	sub. 3	0	Spithead		sub. 3	5	Woodbridge Bar	sub. 3	5
Montrose	sub. 1	5	Queenborough	sub. 1	20	Start Point		add 3	20	Yarmouth Roads	sub. 5	50

the figures, as the case may be, from the time of High Water at London Bridge.

COMPASSES AT GREENHITHE.

compasses. The tide answers for adjusting from 6h. 20m. after the time of high water, until 40m. before the time of be commenced ½-h. and at neap tides 1½-h. earlier than this.

NAME OF DOCK.	Length.	Width.	Water Area.	Depth below T.H.W.	Entrance.				Closed by
					Length	Width.	Depth of sill below T.H.W	Constant for height of high water.*	
	feet.	feet.	acres.	ft. in.	feet.	ft. in.	ft. in.	ft. in.	
EAST INDIA. . . . . IMPORT DOCK	1110	535	17·25	26 0	..	..	..	..	Wood gates ..
,, ,, ... LOCK	..	..	..	..	200	47 5	24 11	+ 4 2	Iron gates ..
,, ,, ... EXPORT DOCK	778	496	7·75	26 0	..	60 0	30 0	+ 9 4	Caisson .. ..
,, ,, BASIN (connecting Import & Export Docks	600 (mean)	191 (mean)	6·50	32 0	..	..	..	..	Wood gates & Iron gates.
,, ,, . . . EASTERN DOCK ENTRANCE	..	..	..	..	210	47 5	24 10	+ 4 2	..
,, ,, . . EASTERN DOCK, LOWER ENTRANCE	..	..	..	..	100	55 0	31 0	+10 4	..
LONDON.	4000	680 (eastern)	40·00	..	..	..	..	..	..
,, ... SHADWELL ENTRANCE (NEW)	..	..	..	..	350	60 0	28 0	+ 7 4	Wood gates ..
,, ... ,, ,, (OLD)	..	..	..	..	180	45 0	24 0	+ 3 4	Composite gates
,, ... WAPPING ENTRANCE	..	..	..	..	170	44 0	23 0	+ 2 4	Wood gates ..
MILLWALL	4500	250	35·50	28 0	..	..	..	..	..
,, ... LOCK	..	..	..	..	450	80 0	28 0	+ 7 4	Iron gates ..
POPLAR	750	310			..	..	..	..	..
,, ...	525	750	7·50	..	..	60 0	28 0	− 5 8	..
POPLAR	350	218	..	..	..	34 0	21 0	+ 8 4	Iron gates ..
REGENT'S CANAL	..	..	10·00	..	..	..	..	..	..
,, ,, ... LOCK	..	..	..	..	350	60 0	28 0	+ 7 4	Iron gates ..

* See footnote on page 5.

Length of Quayage.	Number of Jetties.	Number of Cranes.				Proprietors and City Office.	Other particulars.
		Hand.	Steam.	Hydraulic	Electric.		
feet. 5100	8						
,,	,,						
2900	2					London & India Docks Co., 109, Leadenhall Street, E.C.	Situated at Blackwall, the river entrance adjoining Brunswick Pier and the Terminus of the Fenchurch street Railway. Import goods can be delivered from this dock to railway trucks.
,,	,,	54	1	26	,,		
,,	,,						
,,	,,						
11900	3						
,,	,,					London & India Docks Co., 109, Leadenhall Street, E.C.	Adjoining the St. Katharine Docks and united thereto by bridges. The warehouses have a floor area of 4,748,000 feet. The vaults contain room for 105,000 pipes of wine. The wool warehouses occupy a floor area of 1,197,100 feet. The cranes lift up to 25 tons.
,,	,,	15	2	118	,,		
,,	,,						
8800	,,					Millwall Dock Co., Dock House, 1, Railway Place, Fenchurch Street, E.C.	Inside this dock there is a dry dock. There are sheer legs equal to 80 tons. The cranes lift up to 15 tons.
,,	,,	,,	,,	60	,,		
1865	,,	,,	,,	,,	,,	North London Railway Co., Broad Street Station, E.C.	This dock is entered through the Blackwall Basin of the West India Docks. There are hydraulic cranes for discharging coal into railway trucks, and hydraulic tips for barge loading 200 tons (coal) per hour.
628 alongside river.	,,	,,	,,	,,	,,	Midland Railway Co., 13, Aldersgate Street, E.C.	Cranes to lift up to 5 tons. Staithes for shipping coals from 120 to 150 tons per hour.
1600	6					Regent's Canal & Dock Co., Hopetoun House, 5, Lloyd's Avenue, E.C.	Cranes (26 in number) lift up to 6 tons.
,,	,,	,,	,,	,,	,,		

The weight of a Cubic Foot of Fresh Water is 1000 ounces   35·840 Cubic Feet per Ton.
The weight of a Cubic Foot of the densest Sea Water on the British Coast is 1025 ounces   34·966 Cubic Feet per Ton.

NAME OF DOCK.	Length.	Width.	Water Area.	Depth below T.H.W.	Entrance.		Depth of sill at L.W. V.R.M.	Constant for height of high water.	Closed by
					Length	Width.			
	feet.	feet.	acres.	ft. in.	feet.	ft. in.	ft. in.	ft. in.	
ROYAL ALBERT	6600	490	87·00	29·0	..	..	..	..	..
,, ,, ... New Lock	..	..	..	..	550	80 0	26 0	+·18 0	Iron gates ..
,, ,, ... Old Lock	..	..	..	..	550	80 0	24 0	+ 9 4	Iron gates ..
ROYAL VICTORIA	5000	1000	90·00	27·0	..	..	..	..	..
,, ,, ... Lock	..	..	..	..	325	80 0	{ 26 0 outer 25 0 inner }	{ 27 0 + 10 0 }	Iron gates ..
St. KATHARINE . . . . Western (N.∘ 1)	510	470	4·00	..	..	..	..	..	
,, ,, ... Eastern (N.∘ 2)	500	480	4·00	..	..	..	..	..	
,, ,, ... Basin (N.∘ 3)	450	280	2·00	..	..	..	..	..	
,, ,, ... Lock	..	..	..	..	180	45 0	25 0 + 7 4		Wood gates ..
SURREY COMMERCIAL . . . Albion Dock	1150	460	11·50	..	..	50 0	23 0 + 4 4		Iron gates ..
,, ,, . . . Canada Dock	1350	460	18·72	..	..	44 0	27 0 + 6 4		Iron gates ..
,, ,, . . Greenland Dock	2250	460	22·25	..	..	62 0	27 0 + 6 4		
(Entrance to canal by which vessels reach this Dock)									
,, ,, ... Island Dock	480	170	2·50	..	..	50 0	25 0 + 4 4		Iron gates ..
,, ,, ... Lady Dock	770	460	8·50	..	..	36 0	18 6 — 2 0		
,, ,, ... Lavender Lock	..	..	..	..	320	34 0	18 6 — 2 0		
,, ,, ... Norway Dock	880	270	9·75	..	..	41 0	19 0 — 1 8		

* See footnote on page 0

Length of Quayage.	Number of Jetties.	Number of Cranes or Lifts.				Proprietors and City Office.	Other particulars.
		Hand.	Steam.	Hydraulic.	Electric.		
feet. 17250	..	Including Royal Victoria Docks.				London & India Docks Co., 109, Leadenhall Street, E.C.	Inside this dock there are two dry docks. There are two floating cranes, the "Leviathan," capable of lifting 50 tons, and the "Titan," 30 tons. There is a complete system of goods lines. The warehouses and granaries afford a floor area of 5,560,000 feet.
..	..	24	4	208	..		
..	..						
25000	14	Included with Royal Albert Docks.				London & India Docks Co., 109, Leadenhall Street, E.C.	The cranes in this dock lift up to 15 tons. The two floating cranes noted in the particulars of the Royal Albert Dock, are also available for use in this dock.
..	..						
4400	..						
..	..	27	..	55	..	London & India Docks Co., 109, Leadenhall Street, E.C.	The cranes in this dock lift up to 15 tons. The river entrance is near the Tower Bridge.
..	..						
..	..						
3179	..						These docks contain Timber Ponds with a water area of 62 acres for the storage of Floated Timber. Sheds for the storage of wood goods provide room for 61,000 standards of 165 cubic feet. The grain warehouses have storage room for 271,000 quarters. Some of these warehouses are equipped with portable hydraulic cranes on the dock quays for the discharge of cargoes from vessels alongside and delivery into the granaries. The cranes are fitted with Priestman's self-filling and self-discharging buckets, the labour of filling and emptying the buckets being dispensed with. The grain is lifted out of the vessel by the buckets, and delivered into portable hoppers, which travel on rails outside the buildings, and from the hoppers it is passed on to weighing machines. As the grain
3440	..						
5380	..						
1800	..	..	..	..	..	Surrey Commercial Dock Co., 106, Fenchurch Street, E.C.	
2750	..						
..	..						
1840	..						

NAME OF DOCK.	Length.	Width	Water Area.	Depth below T.H.W.	Entrance.		Depth of sill below T.H.W.	Constant for height of high water. *	Closed by	
					Length	Width.				
	feet.	feet.	acres.	ft. in.	feet.	ft. in.	ft. in.	ft. in.		
WEST INDIA *cont.* PASSAGE TO BLACKWALL BASIN	345	60	..	30 0	..	..	..	..	No gates	..
" " BLACKWALL BASIN (Connecting E. end of West India Import & Export Docks)	750 (average)	500 (extreme)	7·5	26 0	..	..	..	..	..	
" " . . . . LOCK	..	..	..	..	4×0	60 0	30 0	+ 9 4	Iron gates	..
" " LIMEHOUSE BASIN (Connecting W. end of West India Import & Export Docks)	350 (average)	170 (extreme)	1·25	29 0	..	..	..	..	..	
" " . . . . SOUTH DOCK	2650	450	26·75	29 0	..	55 0	..	..	Iron gates	..
" " . . . . . . SOUTH DOCK BASIN	600	375	6·00	29 0	..	..	..	..	..	
" " . . . . EASTERN ENTRANCE	..	..	..	..	480	55 0	29 0	+ 8 4	Iron gates	..
" " JUNCTION DOCK (Connecting Blackwall and South West India Dock Basins)	320	150	1·25	25 0	..	..	..	..	..	

* See footnote on page 9.

		Number of Cranes.				Proprietors and City Office.	Other particulars.
ngth of yage.	Number of Jetties.	Hand.	Steam.	Hydraulic	Electric.		
ct.							
.	..						
.	..						
.	..						
00	..						Basin there is a dry dock. There is railway communication with all the principal railway lines. The cranes lift
00	9	120	20	135	1	London & India Docks Co., 109, Leadenhall Street, E.C.	up to 30 tons. There is a floating derrick, "Elephant," capable of lifting 20 tons.
00	..						
.	..						
.	..						

WHARVES AND RIVERSIDE PREMISES ON THE

NORTH SIDE.

WHARF OR PREMISES.	Proprietors.	Where situated.
LONDON BRIDGE.	Corporation of the City of London	King William Street.
LONDON BRIDGE STEPS.	,, ,, ,,	,, ,,
FRESH WHARF	J. Knill & Co...	Lower Thames Street.
COX & HAMMOND'S QUAYS	,, ,, ,,	,, ,, ,,
BOTOLPH WHARF	Nicholson's Wharves, Ltd.	,, ,, ,,
NICHOLSON'S WHARF	,, ,,	,, ,, ,,
BILLINGSGATE FISH MARKET	Corporation of the City of London	,, ,, ,,
CUSTOM HOUSE (UPPER) STAIRS.	,, ,, ,,	,, ,, ,,
CUSTOM HOUSE QUAY	W. C. Laming & Co.	,, ,, ,,
CUSTOM HOUSE (LOWER) STAIRS.	,, ,, ,,	,, ,, ,,
CUSTOM & WOOL QUAYS	Netherland Steam Ship Co...	,, ,, ,,
BREWERS QUAY	J. Barber & Co.	,, ,, ,,
TOWER STAIRS.	,, ,, ,,	,, ,,
THE TOWER	The Crown	Tower Hill.
TOWER BRIDGE.	Corporation of the City of London	Little Tower Hill.
IRONGATE STAIRS.	,, ,, ,,	St. Katharine Street.
IRONGATE & ST. KATHARINE'S WHARVES.	General Steam Navigation Co.	,, ,, ,,
ST. KATHARINE DOCK ENTRANCE.	,, ,, ,,	,, ,, ,,
HARRISON'S WHARF	Page, Son & East	,, ,, ,,
SOUTH DEVON WHARF	South Devon Wharf Co., Ltd.	Lower East Smithfield.

SOUTH SIDE.

WHARF OR PREMISES.	Proprietors.	Where situated.
LONDON BRIDGE.	Corporation of the City of London ...	Borough High Street.
LONDON BRIDGE STEPS.	„ „ „ „ ...	„ „ „
FENNING'S WHARF	Proprietors of Fenning's Wharf	Tooley St., Southwark.
SUN WHARF	Sun & Topping's Wharf, Ltd...	„ „ „
TOPPING'S WHARF.	„ „ „	„ „ „
CHAMBERLAIN'S WHARF	Chamberlain's Wharf, Ltd.	„ „ „
COTTON'S WHARF.	⎰ Proprietors of Hay's Wharf & ⎱	„ „ „
HAY'S DOCK	⎱ Cotton's Wharf ... ... ⎰	„ „ „
HAY'S WHARF.		„ „ „
BATTLE BRIDGE STAIRS	.. ..	⎰ Battle Bridge Lane,
WILLSON'S WHARF.	Hoare, Wilson & Co.	⎱ Tooley Street.
GRIFFIN'S WHARF	Flack, Chandler & Co.	
SOUTH THAMES WHARF.	Boord & Son, Distillers	⎰ Morgan's Lane,
GUN & SHOT WHARF.	Gun & Shot & Griffin's Wharves Co.,Ltd.	⎱ Tooley Street.
SYMON'S WHARF	Hoare, Wilson & Co.	Stoney Lane, Tooley St.
STANTON'S WHARF.	William France, Fenwick & Co., Ltd.	„ „ „
PICKLE HERRING STAIRS	.. ..	Vine Street, Tooley St.
ST. OLAVES WHARF	Beresford & Co.	„ „ „
PICKLE HERRING WHARF.	Hicks, Nash & Co.	⎰ Pickle Herring street,
MARK BROWN'S WHARF	Leach & Co., Ltd...	⎱ Tooley Street.

NORTH SIDE.

WHARF OR PREMISES.	Proprietors.	Where situated.
BRITISH & FOREIGN WHARF	British and Foreign Wharf, Co., Ltd.	Lower East Smithfield.
MILLER'S WHARF	Horne & Co.	,,
ALDERMAN'S STAIRS.		,,
CARRON WHARF.	Carron Co.	,,
LONDON & CONTINENTAL WHARF	,,	,,
ENTRANCE TO HERMITAGE BASIN, LONDON DOCKS.	London & India Docks Co.	,,
HERMITAGE WHARF	London & Edinburgh Shipping Co.	High Street, Wapping
HERMITAGE STAIRS		,,
ACORN WHARF	J. Husband & Co.	,,
GRANITE WHARF	Colonial Wharves, Ltd.	,,
COLONIAL WHARF	Colonial Wharves, Ltd.	,,
GLOBE WHARF	Herm, Peron & Co., Ltd.	,,
SEWARD'S WHARF	Seward Bros., Ltd.	,,
UNION STAIRS		,,
MELBOURNE WHARF	Tidman & Son, Ltd.	,,
SEWARD'S LOWER WHARVES	Seward Bros., Ltd.	,,
STANDARD WHARF	Herm, Peron & Co., Ltd.	,,
WATSON'S WHARF	Watson's Wharf, Ltd.	,,
BLACK EAGLE WHARF	Truman, Hanbury, Buxton & Co.	,,
ALBION & BREWER'S WHARVES	Capes & Self	,,

SOUTH SIDE.

WHARF OR PREMISES.	Proprietors.	Where situated.
DAVIS' WHARF	Brown & Elmslie	Potter's Fields, Tooley Street.
TOWER BRIDGE.	Corporation of the City of London	Tower Bridge Road.
WORCESTER WHARF	William Moon, Carman & Contractor	Shad Thames, Tooley St.
HORSELYDOWN OLD STAIRS		,, ,, ,,
ANCHOR BREWERY	Courage & Co., Ltd.	,, ,, ,,
BUTLER'S WHARF	Butler's Wharf, Ltd.	,, ,, ,,
St. GEORGE'S STAIRS.		,, ,, ,,
HORSELYDOWN WHARF	A. & P. Keen	,, ,, ,,
COVENTRY'S WHARF	G. & H. Green	,, ,, ,,
COLES UPPER WHARF	A. & P. Keen	,, ,, ,,
HORSELYDOWN NEW STAIRS		,, ,, ,,
NEWELLS WHARF	} Bovill & Sons	,, ,, ,,
COLES LOWER WHARF		,, ,, ,,
LANDELL'S WHARF	R. Chambers & Co.	,, ,, ,,
WEST'S WHARF	A. & P. Keen	,, ,, ,,
MESNARD WHARVES	R. Chambers & Co.	,, ,, ,,
STEAM COAL WHARF	M. A. Ray & Sons	,, ,, ,,

NORTH SIDE.

WHARF OR PREMISES.	Proprietors.	Where situated.
HASTIE'S WHARF	R. & J. Hastie	High Street, Wapping
ST. HELEN'S WHARF	Capes & Self	" " "
WAPPING ENTRANCE TO LONDON DOCK.	London & India Docks Co.	" " "
WAPPING OLD STAIRS		"
OLIVER'S WHARF	Proprietors Oliver's Wharf	" " "
GUN WHARF	H. A. Litchfield & Co.	" " "
ST. JOHN'S WHARF	R. G. Hall & Co.	" " "
SAIL LOFTS	R. Jolly & Sons, Sail Makers	" " "
NEW DUNDEE WHARF	Dundee, Perth & London Shipping Co.	" " "
SUFFERANCE WHARF	George Hedges & Son	" " "
EAGLE WHARF	John Cooper	" " "
BALTIC WHARF	F. Claydon & Co.	" " "
WAPPING NEW STAIRS		" " "
OLD ABERDEEN WHARF	Taylor Brothers	" " "
THAMES POLICE STATION	The Metropolitan Police	" " "
ALEXANDER'S BOTTLE WHARF.	Alfred Alexander & Co.	" " "
ST. JOHN'S (F. & G.) WHARF	R. G. Hall & Co.	" " "
EXCELSIOR WHARF	John Walker, Barge Owner	" " "
PHOENIX WHARF	Andrew Walker, Barge Owner	" " "
ANCHOR MILLS WHARF.	English & Colonial Produce Co., Ltd.	" " "

SOUTH SIDE.

WHARF OR PREMISES.	Proprietors.	Where situated.
ST. SAVIOUR'S DOCK	.. ..	Dockhead, Bermondsey
MILL STAIRS.	.. ..	Mill street, "
REED'S WHARF	H. T. Reed & Sons	Bermondsey Wall.
NEWBALD'S WHARF	William Wesson, Ltd., Wood Hoop Merchants.	" "
DEVERILL'S WHARF	G. Hooper & Co.	" "
BARGE BUILDING YARD	W. G. Downing & Sons, Barge Owners	" "
SACK & TARPAULIN WHARF	Starkey, Room & Co., Sack & Tarpaulin Makers.	" "
REED'S LOWER WHARF	H. T. Reed & Sons	" "
SPRINGALL'S WHARF	Chas. Southwell & Co.	" "
PENRHYN WHARF	Roberts, Adlard & Co. Slaters & Tilers	" "
BRUNSWICK WHARF	Wickens, Pease & Co., Ltd.	" "
COAL WHARF	Bermondsey Wharves, Co., Ltd.	" "
EAST LANE WHARF	The London Grist Mills Co.	" "
EAST LANE STAIRS	.. ..	" "
VESTRY WHARF	Bermondsey Borough Council	" "
LOWER EAST LANE WHARF	B. Smith & Sons	" "

NORTH SIDE.

WHARF OR PREMISES.	Proprietors.	Where situated.
SWAN WHARF	D. & W. Gibbs, Ltd.	High Street, Wapping.
TUNNEL PIER	Thames Conservancy	„ „ „
KING HENRY STAIRS		„ „ „
KING HENRY WHARF	R. G. Hall & Co.	„ „ „
TRINITY WHARF		„ „ „
SHARP'S WHARF	Beresford & Co.	„ „ „
BRIDEWELL HOSPITAL ESTATE WHARF	Bridewell Hospital Estate	„ „ „
WAPPING DOCK STAIRS		„ „ „
WAPPING RAILWAY STAT., THAMES TUNNEL		„ „ „
MIDDLETON'S & ST. BRIDE'S WHARF	Butler's Wharf, Ltd.	„ „ „
COMMERCIAL GAS CO.'S WHARF	Commercial Gas Co.	„ „ „
NEW CRANE STAIRS.		„ „ „
METROPOLITAN & NEW CRANE WHARVES.	Anderson, Weber & Smith	„ „ „
SAINT GEORGE'S SUFFERANCE WHARF	Carlo Gatti & Stevenson	Wapping Wall.
SHELL WHARF	Henry Harvey & Co.	„ „
LUSK'S WHARF	Andrew Lusk & Co.	„ „
JUBILEE WHARF	Keen, Robinson & Co., Ltd.	„ „
METROPOLITAN WHARF	Anderson, Weber & Smith	„ „
KING JAMES' STAIRS.		„ „
METROPOLITAN WHARF	Anderson, Weber & Smith	„ „

SOUTH SIDE.

WHARF OR PREMISES.	Proprietors.	Where situated.
UPPER SUNDERLAND WHARF	⎱ T. Addis & Son .. .. ⎰	Bermondsey Wall.
SUNDERLAND SUFFERANCE WHARF.		,, ,,
MONTREAL GRANARIES	John Dudin & Sons	,, ,,
FREE LANDING PLACE	Parish of Bermondsey	,, ,,
GLOBE MILL WORKS	Unoccupied	,, ,,
GRANARIES	G. Bond	,, ,,
FOUNTAIN DRY DOCK & GRIDIRON. . .	Mills & Knight, Shipwrights, Engineers, &c.	,, ,,
DARNELL'S GRANARIES	W. & J. R. Darnell	,, ,,
FOUNTAIN STAIRS	.. ..	,, ,,
FISHER'S WHARF	W. A. Fisher	,, ,,
POWELL'S WHARF	W. Grose & Co	,, ,,
FARRAND'S WHARF	Gardiner & Tidy	,, ,,
CHERRY GARDEN PIER.	Thames Conservancy	,, ,,
LUCAS & SPENCER'S WHARF.	Lucas & Spencer's Wharf, Ltd.	,, ,,
CORBETT'S WHARF.	T. Addis & Son	Rotherhithe Street.
FLOUR MILLS	The London Milling & Baking Co.	,, ,,
PLATFORM WHARF	Robert Candelish & Son, Ltd.	,, ,,

NORTH SIDE.

WHARF OR PREMISES.	Proprietors.	Where situated.
THORP'S WHARF	Cole & Carey	Wapping Wall.
BARGE BUILDING YARD	Nash & Miller, Barge Builders	,, ,,
PELICAN STAIRS		,, ,,
BARGE BUILDING YARD	Allam & Sons, Barge Builders	,, ,,
LONDON DOCK, OLD ENTRANCE	London & India Docks Co.	Glamis Road.
,, ,, SHADWELL ENTRANCE	,, ,,	,, ,,
SHADWELL DOCK STAIRS		Lower Shadwell.
NEW STAR WHARVES, COLD STORAGE	T. L. Knight & Co.	,, ,,
ICE FACTORY AND COLD STORES	Linde British Refrigeration Co., Ltd. (1887).	,, ,,
SHADWELL FISH MARKET	Corporation of the City of London	,, ,,
BELL WHARF STAIRS		,, ,,
COAL WHARF	Charrington, Sells, Dale & Co.	Broad Street, Ratcliff.
FORAGE WHARF	Abbot & Co.	,, ,, ,,
BOWLES' WHARF	{ The United Oils Co. (G. Moore & Sons, Bottle Merchants	,, ,, ,,
THE FREE TRADE WHARF	The Tees Union Shipping Co.	,, ,, ,,
STONE STAIRS		,, ,, ,,
HUBBUCK'S WHARF	T. Hubbuck & Sons, Ltd.	,, ,, ,,
MARINE BREWERY WHARF	Holt & Co.	,, ,, ,,

SOUTH SIDE.

WHARF OR PREMISES.	Proprietors.	Where situated.	
PLATFORM SUFFERANCE WHARF	T. Groves & Son	Rotherhithe Street.	
PLATFORM ENGINEERING WORKS	Wilmot & Cobon, Engineers & Boiler Makers.	,,	,,
PLATFORM STAIRS		,,	,,
ANGEL TAVERN		,,	,,
LONDON COFFEE HOUSE		,,	,,
BARGE BUILDING PREMISES	R. J. Moore, Boat & Barge Builders	,,	,,
ALBION HOUSE	James J. Pink	,,	,,
BARGE BUILDING PREMISES	Geo. Pace, Barge Builder	,,	,,
DOVER CASTLE TAVERN		,,	
KINGS STAIRS		,,	,,
MAST MAKING PREMISES	G. H. Leggett, Mast Maker	,,	,,
BARGE BUILDING PREMISES	H. Pocock, Barge Builder	,,	,,
COLLEGE HOUSE, MISSION HALL	,, ,, ,,	,,	,,
JOLLY WATERMAN TAVERN		,,	,,
TAILOR'S PREMISES	Newman, Tailor	,,	,,
IRONMONGERY STORES	H. Pocock	,,	,,
BRASS FOUNDER & PUMP MAKERS PREMISES	W. Sells	,,	,,

NORTH SIDE.

WHARF OR PREMISES.	Proprietors.	Where situated.
PINCHIN'S WHARF, PAINT AND COLOUR WORKS	Pinchin, Johnson & Co.	Broad Street, Ratcliff.
KEPIER COAL WHARF	Geo. Gowland & Co.	,, ,, ,,
RATCLIFF CROSS STAIRS		Narrow Street, Ratcliff.
RATCLIFF STORM OUTLET SEWER		,, ,, ,,
PHŒNIX UPPER WHARF	Phœnix Wharves, Ltd.	,, ,, ,,
SAIL LOFT	G. T. Crump, Sail Maker	,, ,, ,,
PHŒNIX LOWER WHARF	Phœnix Wharves, Ltd.	,, ,, ,,
TRINITY WHARF	Anglo-American Oil Co.	,, ,, ,,
RATCLIFF CROSS FLOUR MILLS	J. Marriage	,, ,, ,,
GLOBE FLOUR MILLS	W. Moore, Ltd.	,, ,, ,,
LONDON WHARF	Robert Hough	,, ,, ,,
CROWN MILL WHARF	J. Cooper	,, ,, ,,
EAGLE WHARF	T. L. Knight & Co.	,, ,, ,,
NEW SUN SUFFERANCE WHARF	T. L. Knight & Co.	,, ,, ,,
VANE'S WHARF	F. L. Knight & Co.	,, ,, ,,
OPORTO WHARF	J. Cooper	,, ,, ,,
OLD SUN WHARF	J. Cooper	,, ,, ,,
REGENT'S CANAL WHARF	J. Boulret & Co.	,, ,, ,,
CHINNOCK'S WHARF	Tribe & Co.	,, ,, ,,
REGENT'S CANAL CUT	North Metropolitan Railway & Canal Co.	,, ,, ,,

SOUTH SIDE.

WHARF OR PREMISES.	Proprietors.	Where situated.
PREMISES	Unoccupied	Rotherhithe Street.
YARDLEY'S WHARVES	R. T. Smyth & Co.	„ „
MATTHEW'S WHARF	T. Addis & Son	„ „
FOUNTAIN WHARF	F. D. Collen & Sons	„ „
ROTHERHITHE WHARF	Gordon Coombe	„ „
WHARF	Unoccupied	„ „
CANNON WHARF	} Gillman & Spencer, Ltd.	„ „
GORDON WHARF		„ „
PRINCES STAIRS		„ „
PRINCES WHARF	Gillman & Spencer, Ltd.	„ „
TORBAY TAVERN		„ „
ELEPHANT STAIRS		„ „
BARGE BUILDERS PREMISES	Ward & Son, Barge Builders	„ „
BARGE BUILDERS PREMISES	Smith Bros. „ „	„ „
EAST INDIA WHARF	} John Dudin & Sons	„ „
DUDIN WHARF		„ „
THE STAR OMNIBUS CO.'S WHARF	The Star Omnibus Co., Ltd.	„ „
HOPE WHARF	A. J. Gardiner & Son	„ „

NORTH SIDE.

WHARF OR PREMISES.	Proprietors.	Where situated.		
REGENT'S CANAL ENTRANCE.	North Metropolitan Railway & Canal Co.	Narrow Street, Ratcliff.		
VICTORIA WHARF	Schwartz Bros.	Narrow St., Limehouse.		
LEE CUT	Lee Conservancy.	"	"	"
BRIDGE DRY DOCK	Not now in use	"	"	"
DOVER WHARF	Pintsch's Patent Lighting Co., Ltd.	"	"	"
KIDNEY STAIRS		"	"	"
JUBILEE WHARF.	The Excavator Co., Ltd.	"	"	"
BLYTH'S WHARF.	J. Richardson	"	"	"
WEST'S WHARF	C. R. West	"	"	"
WATERS' WHARF	R. Waters, Lighterman	"	"	"
GRAPE WHARF	Hyman Bros.	"	"	"
HARBOUR MASTER'S OFFICE	The Thames Conservancy	"	"	"
BROADWAY WHARF	Thomas Mason	"	"	"
ETHERIDGE'S WHARF	Geo. Etheridge	"	"	"
BARNETT'S WHARF	James Barnett	"	"	"
FIELDER'S WHARF	C. J. Fielder	"	"	"
MAST, OAR & BLOCK MAKERS YARD	G. & W. Lamb	"	"	"
SPARK'S WHARF	W. N. Sparks, Barge Builder	"	"	"
DUKE SHORE STAIRS		"	"	"
McLINE WHARF	Low, Hart & Co.	"	"	"

SOUTH SIDE.

WHARF OR PREMISES.	Proprietors.	Where situated.
HOPE ANCHOR WORKS	C. Carr, Anchor Smith	Rotherhithe Street.
THAMES TUNNEL FLOUR MILLS	White, Tomkins & Courage, Ltd.	,, ,,
CHURCH STAIRS	.. ..	,, ,,
SPREAD EAGLE TAVERN	.. ..	,, ,,
GRICE'S WHARF	G. & H. Green	,, ,,
TUNNEL WHARF	F. Claydon & Co.	,, ,,
WHARF	S. Ginesi & Co., Stone, Marble & Slate Merchants.	,, ,,
BRANDRAM'S WHARF	Gordon Coombe	,, ,,
BARGE BUILDING PREMISES	Hay, Barge Builder	,, ,,
FISHER'S SUFFERANCE WHARF	Fisher's Wharves & Granaries, Ltd.	,, ,,
CUMBERLAND WHARF	T. Groves & Son	,, ,,
CAROLINA WHARF	Talbot Bros., Iron & Wood Barge Builders	,, ,,
HANOVER STAIRS	.. ..	,, ,,
RANSOMES WHARF	} Talbot Bros., Iron & Wood Barge {	,, ,,
NORWAY WHARF	} Builders {	,, ,,
CLARENCE WHARF	S. Ginesi & Co., Stone Merchants	,, ,,
SURREY GAS WORKS	South Metropolitan Gas Co.	,, ,,
SURREY DOCK TAVERN	.. ..	,, ,,

NORTH SIDE.

WHARF OR PREMISES.	Proprietors.	Where situated.
DUKE SHORE WHARF	Stepney Borough Council	Narrow St., Limehouse.
GILBERT WHARF	Robert Hough	,, ,, ,,
ESSEX WHARF	E. J. Hay & Co.	,, ,, ,,
LANARK WHARF	George Angus & Co., Ltd.	,, ,, ,,
ANCHOR WHARF	William Gibbs, Ltd.	,, ,, ,,
LOWER BREWERY WHARF	William Gibbs, Ltd.	,, ,, ,,
HARTNOLL'S WHARF	F. & P. Hartnoll, Barge Builders	,, ,, ,,
BREWERY WHARF	Taylor & Walker	,, ,, ,,
UPPER BREWERY WHARF	William Gibbs, Ltd.	,, ,, ,,
DUNBAR WHARF	F. V. Smythe & Co.	,, ,, ,,
DUNBAR WHARF	Lamb, Beal & Son	,, ,, ,,
ST. DUNSTANS' WHARF	Gardner & Gardner	,, ,, ,,
DUNBAR WHARF	F. V. Smythe & Co.	,, ,, ,,
LUTON WHARF	Arthur Scott	,, ,, ,,
LIMEHOUSE WHARF	J. & R. Wilson & Co.	,, ,, ,,
LIMEKILN WHARF	R. Passmore & Co.	Three Coit Street,
DUNDEE WHARF	Dundee, Perth & London Shipping Co.	Limehouse.
PIER WHARF	White Tomkins & Courage, Ltd.	Emmett Street, Poplar.
LIMEHOUSE PIER	Thames Conservancy	,, ,, ,,

SOUTH SIDE.

WHARF OR PREMISES.	Proprietors.	Where situated.
SURREY DOCK WHARF	F. Porter & Co., Mill Stone Makers . .	Rotherhithe Street.
SURREY CANAL STAIRS	. . . .	" "
ENTRANCE TO SURREY CANAL DOCK . .	Surrey Commercial Dock Co.	" "
DINORWIC SLATE WHARF	John Williams & Co.	" "
SURREY COMMERCIAL WHARF	G. & H. Green	" "
ROTHERHITHE VESTRY WHARF & WET DOCK	Vestry of Rotherhithe	" "
BELLAMY'S WHARF, KING & QUEEN GRANARIES .	Bellamy's Wharf, Ltd.	" "
KING & QUEEN STAIRS.	. . . .	" "
KING & QUEEN TAVERN	. . . .	" "
KING & QUEEN WHARF	W. B. Dick & Co., Ltd.	" "
KING & QUEEN BARGE WORKS	W. Cory & Son, Ltd., Barge Builders...	" "
PRINCES' DRY DOCK	Princes' Dry Dock Co., Ltd.	" "
C. H. MOWLL	Coal Merchant	" "
UPPER GLOBE WHARF	The Dessicated Grain Co., Ltd. . . .	" "
GLOBE WHARF	A. & P. Keen	" "
GLOBE PIER	Thames Conservancy	" "
GLOBE STAIRS	. . . .	" "
GLOBE WHARF	B. Bogg & Son	" "
GLOBE PIER WHARF	C. H. Grindell & Co.	" "
NORMANDY WHARF, CROWN LEAD WORKS	Quirk, Barton & Co.	" "

NORTH SIDE.

WHARF OR PREMISES.	Proprietors.	Where situated.
LIMEHOUSE WHARF	Venesta Ltd.	Emmett Street, Poplar.
PUBLIC RIGHT OF WAY		,,　　　,,
ABERDEEN WHARF	Aberdeen Steam Navigation Co.	,,　　,,　　,,
ABERDEEN DOCK	Aberdeen Steam Navigation Co.	,,　　,,　　,,
EMMETT STREET FOUNDRY WHARF	T. Smith & Co., Ltd.	,,　　,,　　,,
WEST INDIA DOCK ENTRANCE	London & India Docks Co.	Bridge Road, Poplar.
THAMES WHARF	Jas. Fox & Co.	,,　　,,　　,,
LEAD WORKS	Locke, Lancester & W. W. & R. Johnson & Sons, Ltd.	,,　　,,　　,,
UNION DRY DOCKS	Fletcher, Son & Fearnall, Ltd.	,,　　,,　　,,
CHAIN & ANCHOR WHARF	Lamb, Beal & Son	,,　　,,　　,,
LIMEHOUSE ENTRANCE TO S. W. I. DOCK.	London & India Docks Co.	,,　　,,　　,,
PRIVATE STAIRS BELONGING TO DOCK CO.		West Ferry Rd., Poplar.
MORTON'S SUFFERANCE WHARF	C. & E. Morton	,,　　,,　　,,
MORTON'S RIVER SIDE WHARF		,,　　,,　　,,
WEST INDIA DOCK PIER & STAIRS	Thames Conservancy	,,　　,,　　,,
BATSON'S WHARF, STEAM SAW MILLS, &c.	John Lenanton	,,　　,,　　,,
REGENT'S WHARF	Chas. Price & Co.	,,　　,,　　,,
REGENT DRY DOCK	Glengall Iron Works Co.	,,　　,,　　,,
COUBRO & SCRUTTON'S WHARF	Coubro & Scrutton, Shipwrights, &c.	,,　　,,　　,,

SOUTH SIDE.

WHARF OR PREMISES.	Proprietors.	Where situated.
HORSEFERRY DRY DOCK	J. McDowall & Co., Engineers & Shipwrights	Rotherhithe Street.
HORSEFERRY STAIRS	.. ..	,,　,,
GRAND SURREY WHARF	C. Barry & Co.	,,　,,
LAVENDER DOCK WHARF	Antwerp Traffic & Lavender Dock Wharf Co., Ltd.	,,　,,
LAVENDER WHARF	W. B. Dick & Co., Ltd.	,,　,,
LAVENDER DOCK ENTRANCE	Surrey Commercial Dock Co. ..	,,　,,
PAGEANTS WHARF	Freebody & Co.	,,　,,
PAGEANTS STAIRS	.. ..	,,　,,
UPPER ORDNANCE WHARF	H. J. Enthoven & Sons, Ltd.	,,　,,
WHARF	Unoccupied	,,　,,
LOWER ORDNANCE WHARF	Union Oil & Cake Mills, Ltd.	,,　,,
CUCKOLDS POINT	.. ..	,,　,,
HORNS STAIRS	.. ..	,,　,,
CANADA WHARF	} White, Tomkins & Courage .. } G. & H. Green.. .. .. .. }	,,　,,
NELSON DRY DOCK & SLIP	Mills & Knight, Shipwrights, Engineers, &c.	,,　,,
DANZIC WHARF	Perkins & Homer	,,　,,

NORTH SIDE.

WHARF OR PREMISES.	Proprietors.	Where situated.
OAK WHARF	W. Garner & Sons, Millstone Builders, &c. .. .. J. Crickmore, Barge Builder & Repairer	West Ferry Rd., Poplar
TORRINGTON STAIRS.	.. ..	,, ,, ,,
LONDON WHARF	The Foreign Bottle Manufacturing Co.	,, ,, ,,
BULLIVANT & CO'S WHARF	Bullivant & Co., Ltd., Wire Rope Makers..	,, ,,
HUTCHINGS' WHARF	GRIDIRON, Squire & Calver .. A. S. Flaxman & Co. .. .. T. F. Mohr	,, ,,
BRATT'S WHARF	Bratt's Stave & Cask Syndicate, Ltd..	,, ,,
EMPIRE WORKS	Levy Bros. & Knowles, Ltd., Sack & Bag Merchants..	,, ,,
MOIETY WHARF	The Steam Packing & Engineer's Sundries Co., Ltd.	,, ,, ,,
FISHER'S WHARF	Flower & Everett, Barge Builders ..	,, ,, ,,
LION WHARF	"AXIOM" ENGINEERING WORKS J. Shelborne, Barge Builder ..	,, ,,
ELECTRICAL POWER STORAGE CO'S WHARF	Electrical Power Storage Co	,, ,, ,,

SOUTH SIDE.

WHARF OR PREMISES.	Proprietors.	Where situated.
BARGE BUILDING PREMISES.	J. & P. R. Chadhs, Barge Builders ..	Rotherhithe Street.
SOMERSET WHARF.	T. Faldo, British & Foreign Asphadt Works	,, ,,
LAWRANCE'S WHARF, SURREY RICE MILLS.	Lawrence & Co.	,, ,,
BURT'S WHARF	Burt, Boulton & Hayward, Timber Merchants	,, ,,
TRINITY WHARF.	Trinity Wharf Co.	,, ,,
SOUTH WHARF & PIER	Metropolitan Asylum Board	,, ,,
BARNARD'S WHARF	T. Gabriel & Sons..	,, ,,
COMMERCIAL DOCK PIER	Thames Conservancy	,, ,,
COMMERCIAL DOCK STAIRS	.. ..	,, ,,
COMMERCIAL PIER WHARF	Kemp, Collins & Co., Importers of Timber & Spars	Odessa St., Rotherhithe
CONDEMNED HOLE	H.M. Customs	,, ,,
ATKIN'S WHARF.	} John Dudin & Sons..	,, ,,
ODESSA WHARF		,, ,,
WHITENING STAIRS. (Closed.)	.. ..	,, ,,
BARGE BUILDING PREMISES	Watts, Boat & Barge Builder	,, ,,
GREENLAND DOCK ENTRANCE	Surrey Commercial Dock Co. ..	Dock Alleys, Rother-
BARGE BUILDING PREMISES	Crighton, Barge Builder	,, hithe.

NORTH SIDE.

WHARF OR PREMISES.	Proprietors.	Where situated.
UNION IRON WORKS	S. Hodge & Sons Ltd., Engineers	West Ferry Rd., Poplar
GLENGALL DRY DOCK	Glengall Iron Works, Ltd.	,, ,,
KING'S ARMS STAIRS		,, ,,
ENGINEER & SHIP STORES	Robert Walker	,, ,,
ATLAS CHEMICAL WORKS	J. B. Lawes & Co., Ltd.	,, ,,
TIMOTHY'S WHARF	C. & H. Green	,, ,,
IRON TANK WORKS	Burney & Co.	,, ,,
MELLISH'S WHARF	The London Oil Storage Co.	,, ,,
FENNER'S WHARF, OIL MILLS & COLOUR WORKS	N. J. Fenner & Co.	,, ,,
ENTRANCE TO MILLWALL DOCKS	Millwall Dock Co.	,, ,,
PHŒNIX WHARF, PAINT WORKS	Alex. Duckham & Co.	,, ,,
FLEMING'S WHARF, OIL & CHEMICAL WORKS	Fleming's Oil & Chemical Co., Ltd.	,, ,,
PAINT WORKS	Snowden, Son & Co.	,, ,,
WINKLEY'S WHARF	Mark H. Winkley & Co.	,, ,,
CYCLOPS IRON WORKS	Edward le Bas & Co.	,, ,,
VICTORIA WHARF	Crosse & Blackwell, Provision Merchants	,, ,,
CHAIN & ANCHOR WORKS	Brown, Lennox & Co.	,, ,,
CUTLER'S WHARF, PROVIDENT IRON WORKS	Samuel Cutler & Sons	,, ,,
FERGUSON'S WHARF	Vacuum Oil Co., Ltd.	,, ,,

SOUTH SIDE.

WHARF OR PREMISES.	Proprietors.	Where situated.
DOG & DUCK STAIRS		Dock Alleys, Rother-
BARGE BUILDING PREMISES	Crighton, Barge Builder	" Inthe
SOUTH LOCK ENTRANCE	Surrey Commercial Dock Co.	"
MANGANESE BRONZE & BRASS WORKS	Manganese Bronze & Brass Co., Ltd.	"
GEORGES STAIRS		"
DEPTFORD WHARF & DOCK	The London, Brighton & South Coast Railway Co.	Grove St., Rotherhithe
ROYAL VICTORIA VICTUALLING YARD	The Admiralty	Grove St., Deptford.
FOREIGN CATTLE MARKET, 3 JETTIES	Corporation of the City of London	"
UPPER WATERGATE STAIRS		Watergate St., Deptford
THAMES BOILER WORKS	Thames Iron Works, Shipbuilding & Engineering Co., Ltd., late John Penn & Sons, Ltd.	" "
ENGINEERING WORKS	Humphrys, Tennant & Co., Engineers	Butcher Row, Deptford
LOWER WATERGATE STAIRS & DRAW DOCK		" "
ENGINEERING WORKS	Humphrys, Tennant & Co., Engineers	" "
METROPOLITAN DRY DOCK & GRIDIRON	(General S.N. Co.), The Deptford Dry Docks Co., Ltd.	Deptford Green.
DEPTFORD GREEN DRY DOCK	The Deptford Dry Docks Co., Ltd.	" "
SAWING & DESICCATING WORKS	Holland & Hannen	The Stowage, Deptford

NORTH SIDE.

WHARF OR PREMISES.	Proprietors.	Where situated.		
ROSE'S WHARF, OIL REFINERY	Sir W. A. Rose & Co.	West Ferry Rd., Poplar.		
ST. ANDREWS UNION WHARF	Young & Marten, Ltd., Wholesale Builders, &c.	,,	,,	,,
BRITANNIA DRY DOCK	W. C. Reeder & Co.	,,	,,	,,
COCOANUT STAIRS CAUSEWAY		,,	,,	,,
CASK WORKS	Guelph Patent Cask Co., Ltd.	,,	,,	,,
NAPIER YARD.	Joseph Westwood & Co., Ltd., Engineers	,,	,,	,,
SHIPBUILDING YARD	Edwards & Co., Ltd., Ship Builders & Engineers	,,	,,	,,
MILLWALL METAL CO.'S WORKS	W. P. Renshaw & Co.	,,	,,	,,
BURRELL'S WHARF, COLOUR, OIL & VARNISH WORKS	Burrell & Co.	,,	,,	,,
MILLWALL IRON WORKS	James Livingston & Son	,,	,,	,,
MACONOCHIE BROS. WHARF.	Maconochie Bros., Ltd., Provision Merchants	,,	,,	,,
NELSON'S WHARF	The United Asbestos Co., Ltd. / Hendra & Hammond, Iron & Brass Founders	,,	,,	,,
DISINFECTANT FLUID WORKS	Sir Wm. Burnett	,,	,,	,,
LANGBOURNE WHARF, PAINT WORKS	Duggan, Noel & McColn, Ltd.	,,	,,	,,
THE LONDON CONSTRUCTIVE IRON & BRIDGE WORKS	Matthew T. Shaw & Co., Ltd.	,,	,,	,,

SOUTH SIDE.

WHARF OR PREMISES.	Proprietors.	Where situated.
STOWAGE WHARF	The London Electric Supply Corporation, Ltd.	The Stowage, Deptford.
SHIP & ENGINE REPAIRING WORKS	General Steam Navigation Co.	,, ,, ,,
DEPTFORD CREEK	.. ..	{ Creek Rd., Deptford. { Bridge St., Greenwich.
GAS WORKS	South Metropolitan Gas Co.	Thames St., Greenwich.
SHIPBUILDING YARD	G. Rennie & Co., Shipbuilders	,, ,,
IRON TANK WORKS	G. A. Harvey & Co.	,, ,,
BARGE BUILDING YARD	J. Dards, Barge Builder	Wood Wharf, Green-
WOOD WHARF	Soundy & Son	,, ,, wich.
GREENWICH & ISLE OF DOGS FERRY	(Closed)	,, ,, ,,
FERRY WHARF	D. Noakes & Sons, Forage Factors ..	,, ,, ,,
BARGE BUILDING YARD	Adams & Ashdown, Barge Builders ..	,, ,, ,,
BARGE REPAIRING PREMISES	Doo Bros., Barge Owners..	,, ,, ,,
SUN WHARF	T. R. Huntley, Coal Merchant	,, ,, ,,
BARGE BUILDING YARD	H. B. Burnett & Co., Barge Builders ..	,, ,, ,,
WOOD'S FORAGE WHARF	Wood & Co., Hay & Straw Merchants	,, ,, ,,
BARGE BUILDING YARD	W. G. Allen & Sons, Ltd., Barge Builders	,, ,, ,,
BILLINGSGATE DOCK WHARF	D. Noakes & Sons	,, ,, ,,

NORTH SIDE.

WHARF OR PREMISES.	Proprietors.	Where situated.
MIDLAND OIL WHARF	Millwall Oil Co., Henry Clark & Sons, Ltd., ...	West Ferry Rd., Poplar.
MILLWALL LEAD WORKS	Locke, Lancaster & W. W. & R. } Johnson & Sons, Ltd. .. .. .. }	,, ,, ,,
THE LONDON LEAD SMELTING CO., LTD.. . . .		,, ,, ,,
VIDAL ANILINE DYE WORKS	Vidal Aniline Dye Co. .. .. }	Factory Place, Ferry
OIL MILLS	Owen Parry, Ltd. .. .. }	Street Poplar.
GREENWICH & ISLE OF DOGS FERRY .	Closed	West Ferry Rd., Poplar.
PORT OF LONDON WHARF	Thames Conservancy	,, ,, ,,
MILLWALL BOILER WORKS	Jno. Fraser & Son, Steam Boiler Manufacturers..	
HORSE SHOE & NAIL WORKS	The United Horse Shoe & Nail Co., Ltd.	,, ,, ,,
JOHNSTON'S DRAW DOCK		
NORTH GREENWICH RAILWAY TERMINUS & PIER	Great Eastern Railway Co...	,, ,, ,,
GREENWICH & ISLE OF DOGS PEDESTRIAN SUBWAY	London County Council..	Wharf Road, Poplar.
ISLAND GARDENS (opposite R.N. College, Greenwich)	London County Council..	,, ,,
BARREL WHARF.	Thames Steam Cooperage Co.	,, ,, ,,
JARRAHDALE WHARF	The Cubitt Town Wharves & Saw Mills, Ltd.	,, ,, ,,
SLATE WHARF	T. & J. H. Stirling, Slate Merchants	,, ,, ,,
CUMBERLAND OIL MILLS	George Armstrong & Co., Ltd.	,, ,, ,,

SOUTH SIDE.

WHARF OR PREMISES.	Proprietors.	Where situated.
BILLINGSGATE DRAW DOCK		Billingsgate St.,
COAL WHARF	T. R. Huntley, Coal Merchant	Greenwich.
FUBB'S YACHT TAVERN		Brewhouse Lane,
PRIVATE HOUSES		Greenwich.
GREENWICH AND ISLE OF DOGS PEDESTRIAN SUBWAY	London County Council	Church St., Greenwich.
GARDEN STAIRS		,, ,, ,,
SHIP TAVERN		King William Street,
GREENWICH PIER	Greenwich Pier Co.	Greenwich.
ROYAL NAVAL COLLEGE, Greenwich	The Admiralty	Romney Rd, Greenwich
TRAFALGAR TAVERN		East Greenwich.
YACHT TAVERN		,, ,,
YACHT BOAT HOUSE	E. Freak, Boat Proprietor	,, ,,
BOAT HOUSE	Corbett, Boat Builder	,, ,,
HIGH BRIDGE DRAW DOCK		,, ,,
THREE CROWNS TAVERN		,, ,,
GREENWICH CONSERVATIVE CLUB HOUSE (Crown & Sceptre Tavern)		,, ,,
BOAT HOUSE	Curlew Rowing Club	,, ,,
TRINITY HOSPITAL	Trustees, Mercers' Company	,, ,,

NORTH SIDE.

WHARF OR PREMISES.	Proprietors.	Where situated.
CHRISTCHURCH DRAW DOCK	.. ..	Wharf Road, Poplar.
GROSVENOR WHARF	The Petrofite Fuel Syndicate, Ltd. ..	,, ,, ,,
ALPHA WHARF	Colthurst & Harding	, ,, ,,
POPLAR DRY DOCK	Brown's Dry Dock & Engineering Co., Ltd.	,, ,, ,,
OIL, COLOUR & VARNISH WORKS.	Wilkinson, Heywood & Clark, Ltd., David Storer & Sons	,, ,, ,,
CUBITT TOWN DRY DOCK	Rait & Gardiner, Shipwrights, Engineers & Boiler Makers	,, ,, ,,
CUBITT TOWN WHARF	The Cotton Seed Co., Ltd.	,, , ,,
PLYMOUTH WHARF	Deane, Ransome & Co., Ltd., Constructional Engineers	,, ,, ,,
PYRIMONT WHARF.	Claridge's Patent Asphalt Co., Ltd. ..	,, ,, ,,
DUDGEON'S WHARF	The London Oil Storage Co., Ltd. ..	Manchester Rd., Poplar.
CUBITT TOWN PIER. (Closed.)	.. ..	,, ,, ,,
MILLWALL WHARF.	James W. Cook & Co., Ltd.	,, ,, ,,
SHIPBUILDING & ENGINEERING WORKS.	Yarrow & Co., Ltd., Engineers & Shipbuilders	,, ,, ,,
WOOD VULCANIZING WORKS	The Haskin Wood Vulcanizing Co.	,, ,, ,,
WRINGING MACHINE MANUFACTORY	The Sterling Manufacturing Co., Ltd.	Stewart Street, Poplar.
PERAMBULATOR MANUFACTORY	Star Manufacturing Co., Ltd.	,, ,, ,,
DRAW DOCK	.. ..	,, ,, ,,

SOUTH SIDE.

WHARF OR PREMISES.	Proprietors.	Where situated.
CROWLEY'S WHARF } GOLDEN ANCHOR WHARF } L.C.C. Tramway Depôt.	London County Council..	East Greenwich.
GOLDEN ANCHOR STAIRS	.. ..	,, ,,
ANCHOR WHARF.	C. A. Robinson, Iron & Metal Merchant	,, ,,
UNION STAIRS	.. ..	,, ,,
UNION WHARF	{ W. Budd .. .. } { Thames Conservancy .. .. .. }	,, ,, ,, ,,
GREENWICH WHARF	John Waddell & Sons, Coal Merchants	,, ,,
CEMENT WHARF.	William Whiteway & Co., Cement, Lime & Brick Manufacturers.. ..	,, ,,
GREENOCK WHARF	John Mowlem & Co's Stone Works..	,, ,,
PARISH WHARF	Greenwich District Board of Works.	,, ,,
PROVIDENCE WHARF.	F. A. Hughes, Barge Builder	,, ,,
PIPER'S WHARF	J. Piper, Shipwright & Barge Builder	,, ,,
DAWSON'S WHARF	G. Christopherson, Barge Builder ..	,, ,,
ENDERBY'S WHARF, TELEGRAPH WORKS	Telegraph Construction & Maintenance Co., Ltd..	,, ,,
THAMES SOAP WORKS & GREENWICH SPERM CANDLE WORKS	Wilkie & Soames, Ltd.	,, ,,
PORTLAND CEMENT WORKS.	Hollick & Co., Ltd. (Closed)	,, ,,

NORTH SIDE.

WHARF OR PREMISES.	Proprietors.	Where situated.
EBNER'S WHARF	J. F. Ebner, Parquet, Wood Block & Mosaic Manufacturer	Stewart Street, Poplar.
PREMISES TO LET	Union Lighterage Co., Ltd.	,, ,,
ENGINE WORKS	John Stewart & Son, Ltd., Engineers,	,, ,,
TUG BUILDING & REPAIRING YARD	William Watkins, Tug Owner	Folly Wall, Poplar.
STEWART'S WHARF	John Stewart & Son Ltd., Shipbuilders	,, ,,
CANAL DRY DOCK	John Stewart & Son, Ltd., Engineers & Shipbuilders	Manchester Rd., Poplar.
SOUTH (WEST INDIA) DOCK ENTRANCE.	London & India Docks Co.	,, ,,
CONCORDIA WHARF	C. G. Tindal	Cold Harbour, Poplar.
THAMES POLICE STATION.	Metropolitan Police	,, ,,
NORTH WHARF	Metropolitan Asylum Board	,, ,,
CROWN WHARF	W. Williams, Barge Builder	,, ,,
WEST INDIA DOCK ENTRANCE.	London & India Docks Co.	Preston's Road, Poplar.
BLACKWALL TUNNEL (Pedestrian entrance)	London County Council	,, ,,
RALEIGH PARK for Women and Children	London County Council	Rafeana Road, Poplar.
BLACKWALL CAUSEWAY		Brunswick St., Poplar.
POPLAR DOCKS	Midland Railway Co.	,, ,,
BLACKWALL YARD	R. & H. Green, Ltd., Shipbuilders & Engineers	,, ,,
BLACKWALL STAIRS. (Closed.)		Blackwall.
BLACKWALL PIER & RAILWAY TERMINUS	Great Eastern Railway Co.	,,

SOUTH SIDE.

WHARF OR PREMISES.	Proprietors.	Where situated.
MORDEN WHARF	The Thames White Lead Co., Ltd...	East Greenwich.
CEMENT WORKS	William Ashby & Sons, Ltd...	,, ,,
BOILER WORKS	Maudslay, Sons & Field, Ltd., Engineers	,, ,,
LINOLEUM MANUFACTORY, VICTORIA WORKS . .	The Greenwich Inlaid Linoleum Co., Ltd.	,, ,,
THE THAMES SILICATED STONE WORKS	Imperial Stone Co., Ltd...	,, ,,
SUSSEX WHARF, BLOCK FUEL & DISINFECTING WORKS	Forbes, Abbott & Lennard, Ltd. ..	,, ,,
SAW MILLS & CREOSOTING WORKS	The Improved Wood Pavement Co.,Ltd.	,, ,,
THE FIRE PROOF FLOORS & CONSTRUCTIONAL IRON & STEEL WORKS.	Mark Fawcett & Co., Engineers	,,
LINOLEUM MANUFACTORY	The Greenwich Inlaid Linoleum Co., Ltd.	,, ,,
BELL'S ASBESTOLINE MANUFACTORY	Bell & Co.	,, ,,
TUNNEL WHARF	H. Shrubsall, Barge Builder	,, ,,
ICE FACTORY	The North Pole Ice & Refrigerating Co., Ltd.	,, ,,
POINT WHARF	A. R. Edmonds & Co., Barge Repairers	Blackwall Point.
BLACKWALL TUNNEL (Pedestrian entrance) . . .	London County Council..	,, ,,
POINT DRAW DOCK		,, ,,
ORDNANCE WHARF, TAR WORKS	Forbes, Abbott & Lennard, Ltd. ..	,, ,,
BLACKWALL POINT DRY DOCK	John Stewart & Son, Ltd., Engineers.	,, ,,

D

NORTH SIDE.	Where situated.	Depth of water at Low Water Mark at ordinary Spring tide on same date	Number of vessels which can be moored in one tier	*Number of Buoys on each
		Feet.		
1. TOWER STAIRS, UPPER STEAM TIER	Off Tower Stairs	12	2	..
2. TOWER STAIRS, LOWER STEAM TIER	" "	11	2	..
3. ST. KATHARINES STEAM TIER	Off Irongate Stairs	12	2	..
4. ALDERMAN'S STEAM TIER	Off Alderman's Stairs	15	2	..
5. HERMITAGE, UPPER STEAM TIER	Off Hermitage Stairs	16	2	..
6. HERMITAGE, LOWER STEAM TIER	" "	13	2	..
7. UNION STAIRS, UPPER STEAM TIER	Off Union Stairs	14	2	..
8. UNION STAIRS, LOWER STEAM TIER	" "	14	2	..
9. BELL WHARF TIER	Off Bell Wharf Stairs	14	2	..
10. STONE STAIRS TIER	Off Stone Stairs	14	2	1
11. RATCLIFF CROSS TIER	Off Ratcliff Cross Stairs	12	2	1
12. WEST INDIA DOCK TIER	Off Union Dry Docks	18	2	2
13. CUBITT TOWN TIER	Off Dudgeon's Wharf	17	2	2
14. FOLLY HOUSE TIER	Off Millwall Wharf	22	1	2
15. TIER OFF YARROW & CO.'S YARD	Off Yarrow & Co.'s Yard	14	2	2
16. PLAISTOW, UPPER COASTER TIER	Below Royal Victoria Docks	12	1	1
17. PLAISTOW, LOWER COASTER TIER	" " "	15	1	2

* The moorings which have no Buoys are fitted with ground chains. The boatmen who attends to the mooring of vessels pays for the chains for mooring.

SOUTH SIDE.	Where situated.	Depth of water at Low Water Mark of ordinary Spring Tides. accommodate	Number of vessels which each Tier can	Number of Buoys (if any).
		Feet.		
1. BATTLE BRIDGE, UPPER STEAM TIER	Off Battle Bridge Stairs	12	2	..
2. BATTLE BRIDGE, LOWER STEAM TIER	„ „ „ „	13	2	..
3. GEORGE'S STAIRS, UPPER STEAM TIER	Off St. George's Stairs	15	2	2
4. GEORGE'S STAIRS, LOWER STEAM TIER	„ „ „	15	2	2
5. MILL STAIRS STEAM TIER	Off Mill Stairs	15	2	..
6. EAST LANE, UPPER STEAM TIER	Off East Lane Stairs	16	2	..
7. EAST LANE, LOWER STEAM TIER	„ „ „	14	2	..
8. FOUNTAIN HOLE STEAM TIER	Off Fountain Stairs	11	2	..
9. PLATFORM TIER	Off Platform Stairs	12	2	..
10. PRINCES STAIRS, UPPER TIER	Off Princes Stairs	14	4	..
11. PRINCES STAIRS, MIDDLE TIER	„ „ „	13	4	..
12. PRINCES STAIRS, LOWER TIER	„ „ „	13	8	..
13. CHURCH HOLE TIER	Off Church Stairs	14	2	..
14. HANOVER HOLE TIER	Off Hanover Stairs	17	2	..
15. MILL HOLE TIER	„ „ „	16	2	..
16. SURREY CANAL TIER	Off King & Queen Stairs	16	2	2
17. DEADMAN'S, OR SOUTH COAST, UPPER TIER	Off Georges Stairs	17	2	2

* The moorings which have no Buoys are fitted with ground chains. The boatman who attends to the mooring of vessels provides the chains for mooring.

d 2

NORTH SIDE.	Where situated.	Depth of water at Low Water Mark of ordinary Spring Tides	Number of vessels which each Tier can accommodate	Number of Buoys (if any).
		Feet.		
18. SILVERTOWN, COASTER TIER	Off Silvertown	16	2	2
19. NORTH WOOLWICH TIER	" " "	16	2	2
20. BECKTON STEAM COLLIER TIER	Off Barking Creek	19	2	3
21. RAINHAM PETROLEUM TIER	Below Rainham Creek	25	1	2

NOTE.—In addition to the above, there are 28 Barge roads on the North side of the River.

SOUTH SIDE.	Where situated.	Depth of water at Low Water Mark of ordinary Spring Tides.	Number of vessels which each Tier can accommodate	Number of Buoys (if any).
		Feet.		
18. DEADMAN'S, OR SOUTH COAST, LOWER TIER	Off Georges Stairs	17	2	2
19. DEPTFORD LOWER TIER	Off Lower Watergate Stairs.	18	2	2
20. DEPTFORD CREEK, UPPER TIER	Off Deptford Creek..	20	2	2
21. DEPTFORD CREEK, LOWER TIER	,, ,, ,, ...	20	2	2
22. GREENWICH PETROLEUM TIER	,, ,, ,, ...	26	1	2
23. CHARLTON, UPPER STEAM COLLIER TIER .	Off Charlton Ballast Wharf.	23	2	2
24. CHARLTON, LOWER STEAM COLLIER TIER .	,, ,, ,, .	22	2	2
25. GALLEONS, UPPER STEAM COLLIER TIER .	Off lower end of Arsenal ..	20	2	2
26. GALLEONS, LOWER STEAM COLLIER TIER .	,, ,, ,, ..	17	2	2
27. HALFWAY REACH, STEAM COLLIER TIER .	Below Main Drainage Outfall	19	2	2
28. ERITH UPPER TIER.	Off Erith	26	2	2
29. GREENHITHE CEMENT SHIP ROAD	Off Greenhithe	30	2	1
30. NORTHFLEET CEMENT SHIP ROAD	Above Northfleet Creek ..	40	1	1
31. HIGHAM RED POWDER BUOY No. 1 . . .	Above Shorn Mead Battery.	26	1	1
32. HIGHAM RED POWDER BUOY No. 2 . . .	,, ,, ,, ,, .	26	1	1
33. HIGHAM RED POWDER BUOY No. 3 . . .	,, ,, ,, ,, .	26	1	1
34. POWDER BUOY OFF POWDER NOTICE BOARD	Below Gravesend	22	1	1

NOTE.—In addition to the above, there are 34 Barge roads on the South side of the River.

LINES OF VESSELS TO AND FROM LONDON, AND THE DOCKS USED BY THEM ON THE THAMES.

LINES.	OWNERS OR BROKERS.	DOCKS.
ABERDEEN LINE . . . To Australia & South Africa Steamers	G. Thompson & Co., 7, Billiter Square, E.C. . . .	Royal Albert.
ABERDEEN LINE . . . . Sailing Ships		East India.
ABERDEEN LINE . . . . . To & from Port Natal	J. T. Rennie, Son & Co., 3, East India Avenue, E.C.	London.
ALLAN LINE	Allan Brothers & Co., 103, Leadenhall Street, E.C.	Royal Albert.
ANCHOR LINE . . . . From Calcutta	Henderson Brothers, Ltd., Leadenhall Chambers, & 56, Mary Axe, E.C.	Tilbury.
ANDERSON, ANDERSON & CO.'S LINE . . . Sailing Ships to Australia	Anderson, Anderson & Co., 5, Fenchurch Avenue, E.C.	South West India.
ANGLO-AUSTRALASIAN LINE	Anglo-Australasian Steam Navigation Co., 234, Billiter Avenue, E.C.	Royal Victoria.
ANTWERP LINE	Furness, Withy & Co., Ltd., 4, Fenchurch Avenue, E.C.	London.
ARGO STEAMSHIP CO.'S LINE	Argo Steamship Co., 4, Crutched Street, E.C. . .	St. Katharine.
ATLANTIC TRANSPORT LINE . . . England & America	Atlantic Transport Co., 108, Fenchurch Street, E.C.	Tilbury. Royal Albert. West India.
AUSTRALIAN MUTUAL SHIPPING CO.'S LINE . . . . Sailing Ships	Winnall, Cooper & Co., 10 & 11, Lime Street, E.C.	East India.
BAILEY & LEETHAM LINE	Bailey & Leetham, Dunster House, 12, Mark Lane, E.C.	Millwall.
BEN LINE . . . . Inwards	Galbraith, Pembroke & Co., 8, Austin Friars, E.C.	East India.
BEN LINE . . . . Outwards	Killick, Martin & Co., 7, Pen Court, Fenchurch Street, E.C.	South West India.
BIBBY LINE	A. Howden & Co., Rochester Buildings, 158, Leadenhall Street, E.C.	Tilbury.

LINES.	OWNERS OR BROKERS.	DOCKS.
BLUE ANCHOR LINE.	W. Lund, 3, East India Avenue, E.C.	Royal Albert.
BOTT, W. E., & CO.'S LINE . To Gothenburg, Christiana & Riga	W. E. Bott & Co., 1, East India Avenue, E.C. . .	Millwall.
BRITISH INDIA LINE.	British India Steam Navigation Co., British India House, Great Winchester Street, E.C.	Royal Albert.
BRITISH & IRISH S. P. CO.'S LINE . . . . City of Cork S. P. Co.	J. Hartley & Co., 19, Leadenhall Street, E.C. . .	London.
BUCKNALL STEAMSHIP LINES, LTD . . .	Bucknall & Brothers, East India Chambers, 23, Leadenhall Street, E.C.	West India.
CAYO LINE . . . . Cuban S. S. Co., Ltd.	Scrutton, Sons & Co., 9, Gracechurch Street, E.C.	Millwall.
CHINA MUTUAL STEAM NAV. CO.'S LINE	China Mutual Steam Navigation Co., 3, Billiter Avenue, E.C.	South West India.
CITY LINE	Montgomerie & Workman, 36, Gracechurch Street, E.C.	Tilbury.
CITY OF CORK LINE. City of Cork S. P. Co., Ltd.	J. Hartley & Co., 19, Leadenhall Street, E.C. . . .	London.
CLAN LINE	Cayzer, Irvine & Co., 115, Leadenhall street, E.C.	Tilbury.
CLYDE LINE . . To & From Glasgow, Greenock, &c.	Clyde Shipping Co., 138, Leadenhall Street, E.C. . .	St. Katharine.
CUBAN LINE . . . . Cuban S. S. Co., Ltd.	E. Bigland & Co., 7, East India Avenue, E.C. . . .	Millwall.
DEMERARA & BERBICE LINE . . Outwards Inwards .	Demerara & Berbice Steamship Co., 86, Leadenhall street, E.C.	South West India. London.
DEVITT & MOORE'S LINE	Devitt & Moore, 12, Fenchurch Buildings, E.C. . .	East India.
DIRECT LINE. . . . . Steamers	Henry Langridge & Co., 16, Great St. Helen's, E.C.	South West India.
DUCAL LINE	J. B. Westray & Co., 138, Leadenhall Street, E.C. .	Royal Albert.

LINES.	OWNERS OR BROKERS.	DOCKS.
ORIENT-PACIFIC LINE	Orient Steam Navigation, Ltd., 11, Fenchurch, Tilbury. Avenue, E.C.	
P. AND O. LINE	Peninsular & Oriental Steam Navigation Co., 122, Royal Albert. Leadenhall Street, E.C.	
PERLBACH'S LINE . . . . . . London & Hamburg	H. J. Perlbach & Co., 6-8, Fenchurch Street, E.C.	Tilbury.
PHILADELPHIA TRANS-ATLANTIC LINE . .	Sharpe & Squier & Fisher, Leccesy Square, E.C.	West India.
PRINCE LINE, LTD. . To Mediterranean & River Plate	P. Cayo & Co., 8, Fenchurch, Ltd.	Royal Victoria.
QUEEN LINE . The London & Channel Islands S. S. Co. Ltd.	Clarke, Liddle & Ford, 30, Dunstan's buildings, St. Dunstan's Hill, E.C.	London.
RED CROSS LINE. . . C. M. Norwood & Co. . . .	Paul & Stellmacher, 21, Idioter street, E.C. . . .	Millwall.
ROYAL MAIL S. P. CO.'S LINE	Royal Mail Steam Packet Co., 18, Moorgate street.	Royal Victoria.
SCOTTISH LINE . . . . Sailing Ships	Wedgwood, Mcfarlane & Co., Proprietary, Ltd., South West India. 3 & 4, Lime Street Square, E.C.	
SCRUTTON'S LINE . . . . { Outward { Inward	Scrutton, Sons & Co., 9, Gracechurch street, E.C.	South West India. London.
SHAW, SAVILL & ALBION CO.'S { Steamers . . LINE { Sailing Ships	Shaw, Savill & Albion Co., Ltd., 34, Leadenhall. Street, E.C.	Royal Albert. East India.
SHIRE LINE . . . To Australia & New Zealand, Eastern S. S. Co. Ltd. { Outward	Turnbull, Martin & Co., 112, Fenchurch Street, E.C.	Royal Victoria. South West India.
SHIRE LINE . . . . To Straits China & Japan	Jenkins & Co., Ltd. 53, London Wall street, E.C. . . .	Royal Albert.
SPEED LINE . . . . To London Harbour	General Steam Navigation, Maritime Bristol & Co., Irongate London. Wharf, Standard & Old Swan, Glamis Street, E.C.	
STAR LINE	James Polaroy & Co., 8 & 11, Fenchurch Avenue, E.C.	Royal Victoria. Royal Albert.
STETTIN & LONDON STEAMSHIP LINE .	Anderson, Barker & Co., 22, Billiter Street, E.C. . . .	Millwall.

LINES.	OWNERS OR BROKERS.	DOCKS.
STOCKHOLM LINE . . The Stockholm S. S. Co. London & Stockholm	Phillipps & Graves, 10 & 11, Lime street, E.C. W. E. Bott & Co., 1, East India Avenue, E.C.	Millwall.
THOMAS & SON'S LINE . . To & from Brussels	D. C. Thomas & Son, 26-28, Billiter street, E.C. ..	London.
THOMPSON LINE . The London Exchange S. S. Co.	Andrew Low, Son & Co. 7, Fenchurch Avenue, E.C.	Royal Victoria.
THULE LINE . . The Thule S. S. Co. Ltd. London & Gothenburg	Phillipps & Graves, 10 & 11, Lime street, E.C. ..	Millwall.
TYSER LINE, LTD.	Tyser & Co., 18, Fenchurch Avenue E.C. . . .	Royal Albert.
UNION-CASTLE LINE.	Union-Castle Mail Steamship Co., Ltd., Donald Currie & Co., 3 & 4, Fenchurch Street, E.C.	East India. Tilbury.
UNITED STEAMSHIP CO.'S LINE . . London to Libau	Texner, Price & Co., 107, Fenchurch Street, E.C. ..	Millwall.
VICTORIA LINE.	Birt, Potter & Hughes, 2, Fenchurch Avenue, E.C.	South West India.
WEST AUSTRALIAN LINE . . . . . Steamers	Bethell, Gwyn & Co., Billiter Buildings, 22, Billiter street, E.C.	South West India.
WESTCOTT LINE.	Westcott & Laurance, Thorne's Chambers, Ingram Court, Fenchurch Street, E.C.	Millwall.
WHITE STAR LINE, Australian Branch	Ismay, Imrie & Co., 34, Leadenhall Street, E.C. ..	Tilbury.
WILSONS & FURNESS-LEYLAND LINE, LTD. New York	Wilsons & Furness-Leyland Line, Ltd., 34, Leadenhall Street, E.C. Thos. Ronaldson & Co., Ltd., 120, Fenchurch Street, E.C.	Royal Albert. Royal Victoria.

ADMIRALTY KNOTS AND EQUIVALENT STATUTE MILES.

Knots.	·00	·25	·50	·75
1	1·1517	1·4391	1·7270	2·0152
2	2·3035	2·5909	2·8788	3·1667
3	3·4552	3·7424	4·0303	4·3182
4	4·6061	4·8939	5·1818	5·4697
5	5·7578	6·0456	6·3335	6·6212
6	6·9083	7·1959	7·4838	7·7727
7	8·0606	8·3485	8·6364	8·9242
8	9·2121	9·5000	9·7878	10·0758
9	10·3636	10·6518	10·9394	11·2273
10	11·5152	11·8030	12·0910	12·3788
11	12·6667	12·9546	13·2424	13·5303
12	13·8182	14·1061	14·3939	14·6818
13	14·9697	15·2576	15·5455	15·8333
14	16·1212	16·4091	16·6970	16·9848
15	17·2727	17·5606	17·8485	18·1364
16	18·4242	18·7121	19·0000	19·2879
17	19·5757	19·8636	20·1515	20·4394
18	20·7273	21·0152	21·4030	21·5909
19	21·8788	22·1667	22·7545	22·7424
20	23·0303	23·3182	23·8061	23·8939
21	24·1818	24·4697	24·7576	25·0455
22	25·3333	25·6212	25·9091	26·1970
23	26·4848	26·7727	27·0606	27·3485
24	27·6364	27·9242	28·2121	28·5000
25	28·7879	29·0758	29·3636	29·6515

The Statute Mile, 5280 feet.
The Geographical Mile, Admiralty Knot, or Nautical Mile, 6080 feet.
Knots × 8·691 = Knots.
1 Mile × 0·8684 = Land measure.
1 League = 3 Miles.
1 Degree = 60 Geographical, or 69·11 Statute Miles.

STATUTE MILES AND EQUIVALENT ADMIRALTY KNOTS.

		Parts of a Mile.		
Miles	100	25	50	75
1	·8684	1·0855	1·3026	1·5197
2	1·7368	1·9539	2·1711	2·3882
3	2·6053	2·8224	3·0395	3·2566
4	3·4737	3·6908	3·9079	4·1250
5	4·3421	4·5592	4·7763	4·9934
6	5·2105	5·4276	5·6447	5·8618
7	6·0789	6·2961	6·5132	6·7303
8	6·9474	7·1645	7·3816	7·5987
9	7·8158	8·0329	8·2500	8·4671
10	8·6842	8·9013	9·1184	9·3355
11	9·5526	9·7697	9·9868	10·2039
12	10·4211	10·6382	10·8553	11·0724
13	11·2895	11·5066	11·7237	11·9408
14	12·1579	12·3750	12·5921	12·8092
15	13·0263	13·2434	13·4605	13·6776
16	13·8947	14·1118	14·3289	14·5461
17	14·7632	14·9803	15·1974	15·4145
18	15·6316	15·8487	16·0658	16·2829
19	16·5000	16·7171	16·9342	17·1513
20	17·3684	17·5855	17·8026	18·0197
21	18·2368	18·4539	18·6710	18·8882
22	19·1023	19·3224	19·5395	19·7566
23	19·9737	20·1908	20·4079	20·6250
24	20·8421	21·0592	21·2763	21·4934
25	21·7105			22·9618

1 Knot = 1853·1843 Mètres.

1 Kilomètre = 0·5396 Knot.

1 Myriamètre = 5·3962 Knots.

Feet per Minute × 0·99 = Knots per Hour.

1 Fathom = 6 feet.

1 Cable Length = 120 Fathoms.

The Log-line used in H.M. Navy is 8 Furlongs, or 48 feet in length.

TIME AND KNOT

Speed in Knots corresponding to the time occupied by Vessels

Minutes.	Seconds.														
	0	1	2	3	4	5	6	7	8	9	10	11	12	13	14
2	30·000	29·752	29·508	29·268	29·032	28·800	28·571	28·346	28·125	27·907	27·692	27·481	27·273	27·068	26·866
3	20·000	19·890	19·780	19·672	19·565	19·459	19·355	19·251	19·149	19·048	18·947	18·848	18·750	18·653	18·557
4	15·000	14·938	14·876	14·815	14·754	14·694	14·634	14·575	14·516	14·458	14·400	14·343	14·286	14·229	14·173
5	12·000	11·960	11·921	11·881	11·842	11·803	11·765	11·726	11·688	11·650	11·613	11·576	11·538	11·502	11·465
6	10·000	9·972	9·945	9·917	9·890	9·863	9·836	9·808	9·783	9·756	9·730	9·704	9·677	9·651	9·626
7	8·571	8·551	8·531	8·511	8·491	8·471	8·451	8·431	8·411	8·392	8·372	8·353	8·333	8·314	8·295
8	7·500	7·484	7·469	7·453	7·438	7·423	7·407	7·392	7·377	7·362	7·347	7·332	7·317	7·302	7·287
9	6·667	6·654	6·642	6·629	6·618	6·606	6·593	6·584	6·569	6·557	6·545	6·534	6·522	6·510	6·498
10	6·000	5·990	5·980	5·970	5·960	5·950	5·941	5·931	5·921	5·911	5·902	5·892	5·882	5·873	5·865
11	5·455	5·446	5·438	5·430	5·422	5·414	5·405	5·397	5·389	5·381	5·373	5·365	5·357	5·349	5·341
12	5·000	4·993	4·986	4·979	4·972	4·964	4·958	4·952	4·945	4·938	4·932	4·923	4·918	4·911	4·904
13	4·615	4·609	4·603	4·597	4·591	4·586	4·580	4·574	4·568	4·562	4·557	4·551	4·545	4·540	4·534
14	4·286	4·281	4·276	4·270	4·265	4·260	4·255	4·250	4·245	4·240	4·235	4·230	4·225	4·220	4·215

TABLE.

in running the distance of a measured Knot.

						Seconds.									
5	16	17	18	19	20	21	22	23	24	25	26	27	28	29	Minutes.
667	23·471	26·277	26·087	25·890	25·714	25·532	25·352	25·173	25·000	24·828	24·684	24·400	24·324	24·161	2
602	18·367	18·274	18·182	18·090	18·000	17·910	17·822	17·734	17·647	17·561	17·476	17·391	17·308	17·255	3
118	14·062	14·068	13·953	13·890	13·846	13·793	13·740	13·688	13·636	13·585	13·531	13·483	13·433	13·383	4
429	11·392	11·594	11·521	11·455	11·250	11·215	11·180	11·116	11·111	11·077	11·048	11·009	10·976	10·942	5
690	9·574	9·519	9·521	9·450	9·471	9·440	9·421	9·379	9·375	9·351	9·026	9·302	9·278	9·254	6
276	8·207	8·208	8·219	8·200	8·182	8·163	8·145	8·126	8·108	8·080	8·072	8·051	8·036	8·018	7
273	7·258	7·243	7·259	7·214	7·200	7·186	7·171	7·157	7·143	7·129	7·115	7·101	7·087	7·073	8
988	6·475	6·463	6·452	6·440	6·429	6·417	6·406	6·394	6·383	6·372	6·360	6·349	6·338	6·327	9
854	5·841	5·835	5·855	5·810	5·806	5·797	5·784	5·778	5·769	5·764	5·751	5·742	5·708	5·725	10
285	5·298	5·335	5·319	5·304	5·294	5·286	5·279	5·271	5·263	5·296	5·248	5·240	5·233	5·225	11
898	4·801	4·088	4·878	4·471	4·800	4·258	4·768	4·745	4·836	4·832	4·825	4·812	4·812	4·806	12
524	4·522	4·515	4·511	4·500	4·498	4·491	4·488	4·483	4·177	4·472	4·472	4·464	4·455	4·450	13
211	4·200	4·203	4·196	4·191	4·186	4·181	4·176	4·171	4·166	4·182	4·157	4·152	4·147	4·148	14

Speed in Knots corresponding to the time occupied by Vessels

Minutes.						Seconds.									
	0	1	2	3	4	5	6	7	8	9	10	11	12	13	14
2	30·000	29·752	29·508	29·268		28·901	28·571	28·346	28·125	27·907	27·692	27·480	27·273	27·068	26·866
3	20·000	19·780	19·780	19·672	19·355	19·130	17·050	19·231	19·149	19·008	18·947	18·848	18·750	18·652	18·557
4	15·000	14·783	14·876	14·545	14·754	14·000	14·634	14·570	14·500	14·458	14·000	14·343	14·000	14·229	14·173
5	12·000	11·860	11·821	11·844	11·812	11·811	11·764	11·750	11·634	12·053	11·813	11·570	11·538	11·502	11·465
6	10·000	9·972	9·945	9·917	9·890	9·863	9·836	9·810	9·783	9·756	9·730	9·701	9·677	9·651	9·626
7	8·571	8·551	8·531	8·511	8·491	8·471	8·461	8·431	8·411	8·392	8·373	8·353	8·333	8·314	8·295
8	7·500	7·484	7·469	7·453	7·438	7·423	7·406	7·398	7·377	7·362	7·347	7·328	7·317	7·300	7·287
9	6·667	6·654	6·642	6·429	6·548	6·490	6·693	6·381	6·360	6·357	6·345	6·384	6·322	6·310	6·498
10	6·000	5·990	5·940	5·970	5·960	5·950	5·941	5·931	5·623	5·911	5·902	5·892	5·883	5·873	5·863
11	5·454	5·447	5·438	5·430	5·422	5·414	5·406	5·397	5·389	5·381	5·373	5·365	5·357	5·349	5·341
12	5·000	4·993	4·986	4·979	4·972	4·966	4·958	4·952	4·945	4·938	4·932	4·925	4·918	4·911	4·905
13	4·615	4·609	4·603	4·598	4·591	4·586	4·580	4·574	4·568	4·562	4·557	4·551	4·545	4·540	4·534
14	4·285	4·280	4·276	4·270	4·265	4·260	4·255	4·250	4·245	4·240	4·235	4·230	4·226	4·220	4·215

TABLE.
in running the distance of a measured Knot.

						Seconds.									Minutes.
5	16	17	18	19	20	21	22	23	24	25	26	27	28	29	
·667	26·471	26·277	26·087	25·890	25·711	25·532	25·352	25·173	25·000	24·828	24·658	24·490	24·324	24·161	2
·482	18·367	18·274	18·182	18·090	18·000	17·910	17·822	17·734	17·647	17·561	17·476	17·391	17·308	17·225	3
·118	14·062	14·008	13·953	13·900	13·846	13·795	13·740	13·688	13·636	13·585	13·534	13·483	13·433	13·383	4
·429	11·392	11·358	11·321	11·285	11·250	11·215	11·180	11·146	11·111	11·077	11·043	11·009	10·976	10·942	5
·690	9·574	9·549	9·521	9·499	9·474	9·449	9·424	9·399	9·375	9·351	9·326	9·302	9·278	9·254	6
·276	8·257	8·238	8·219	8·200	8·182	8·163	8·145	8·126	8·108	8·090	8·072	8·054	8·036	8·018	7
·273	7·258	7·243	7·229	7·214	7·200	7·186	7·171	7·157	7·143	7·129	7·115	7·101	7·087	7·073	8
·480	6·475	6·462	6·452	6·440	6·429	6·417	6·406	6·394	6·383	6·372	6·360	6·349	6·338	6·327	9
·854	5·844	5·825	5·825	5·816	5·806	5·797	5·788	5·778	5·769	5·760	5·751	5·742	5·732	5·723	10
·333	5·325	5·318	5·310	5·302	5·294	5·286	5·278	5·271	5·263	5·255	5·248	5·240	5·233	5·225	11
·898	4·891	4·885	4·878	4·871	4·865	4·858	4·852	4·845	4·838	4·832	4·825	4·819	4·812	4·806	12
·528	4·522	4·516	4·511	4·505	4·500	4·494	4·489	4·483	4·477	4·472	4·466	4·460	4·455	4·450	13
·211	4·206	4·201	4·196	4·191	4·186	4·181	4·176	4·171	4·166	4·162	4·157	4·152	4·147	4·143	14

TIME AND KNOT

Speed in Knots corresponding to the time occupied by Vessels

Minutes.	Seconds.														
	30	31	32	33	34	35	36	37	38	39	40	41	42	43	44
2	24·000	23·841	23·684	23·529	23·377	23·226	23·077	22·930	22·785	22·642	22·500	22·360	22·222	22·085	21·951
3	17·143	17·002	16·884	16·760	16·622	16·511	16·607	16·390	16·514	16·156	16·361	15·930	16·216	16·142	16·071
4	13·333	13·284	13·223	13·157	13·129	13·004	12·945	12·890	12·950	12·905	12·857	12·811	12·766	12·721	12·676
5	10·909	10·870	10·843	10·811	10·778	10·715	10·714	10·692	10·651	10·612	10·588	10·517	10·526	10·490	10·465
6	9·231	9·507	9·784	9·196	9·157	9·111	9·084	9·058	9·065	9·022	9·000	8·978	8·905	8·852	8·811
7	8·060	7·982	7·964	7·947	7·930	7·912	7·895	7·877	7·800	7·813	7·826	7·809	7·792	7·773	7·759
8	7·059	7·046	7·034	7·015	7·004	6·965	6·977	6·963	6·950	6·936	6·925	6·910	6·897	6·885	6·870
9	6·316	6·305	6·294	6·280	6·272	6·261	6·250	6·239	6·228	6·218	6·196	6·186	6·175	6·164	
10	5·711	5·706	5·696	5·687	5·678	5·665	5·660	5·651	5·615	5·634	5·625	5·616	5·607	5·500	5·580
11	5·217	5·209	5·202	5·195	5·187	5·180	5·172	5·165	5·158	5·150	5·143	5·134	5·128	5·123	5·114
12	4·800	4·793	4·787	4·780	4·774	4·768	4·761	4·756	4·750	4·744	4·737	4·730	4·725	4·718	4·712
13	4·414	4·405	4·403	4·428	4·423	4·417	4·411	4·400	4·400	4·395	4·390	4·383	4·378	4·371	4·363
14	4·167	4·153	4·155	4·154	4·145	4·144	4·139	4·135	4·130	4·095	4·090	4·086	4·081	4·077	4·072

TABLE—continued.
in running the distance of a measured Knot.

						Seconds.									
45	46	47	48	49	50	51	52	53	54	55	56	57	58	59	Minutes.
·518	21·587	21·537	21·423	21·302	21·176	21·055	20·930	20·809	20·690	20·571	20·455	20·339	20·225	20·112	2
·060	15·929	15·859	15·789	15·721	15·652	15·584	15·517	15·451	15·385	15·319	15·254	15·189	15·126	15·063	3
·633	12·587	12·544	12·500	12·457	12·414	12·371	12·329	12·287	12·245	12·203	12·162	12·121	12·081	12·040	4
·433	10·405	10·373	10·343	10·315	10·286	10·256	10·227	10·198	10·169	10·141	10·112	10·084	10·056	10·028	5
·853	8·867	8·845	8·823	8·802	8·780	8·759	8·738	8·717	8·696	8·675	8·654	8·633	8·612	8·592	6
·742	7·725	7·709	7·692	7·676	7·660	7·643	7·627	7·611	7·595	7·579	7·563	7·547	7·531	7·515	7
·857	6·844	6·831	6·818	6·805	6·792	6·780	6·767	6·754	6·742	6·729	6·716	6·704	6·691	6·679	8
·154	6·143	6·133	6·122	6·112	6·102	6·091	6·081	6·071	6·061	6·050	6·040	6·030	6·020	6·010	9
·584	5·575	5·564	5·556	5·547	5·538	5·530	5·521	5·513	5·505	5·496	5·488	5·479	5·471	5·463	10
·106	5·099	5·092	5·085	5·078	5·070	5·063	5·056	5·049	5·042	5·035	5·028	5·021	5·014	5·007	11
·706	4·700	4·694	4·687	4·681	4·675	4·669	4·665	4·657	4·651	4·645	4·639	4·633	4·627	4·621	12
·361	4·356	4·351	4·347	4·342	4·337	4·332	4·327	4·322	4·316	4·311	4·306	4·301	4·296	4·291	13
·068	4·063	4·059	4·054	4·049	4·045	4·040	4·035	4·031	4·027	4·022	4·018	4·013	4·009	4·004	14

E

DISTANCES ON THE RIVER THAMES, MEASURED FROM THE CENTRAL ARCH OF LONDON BRIDGE DOWN THE CENTRE OF THE RIVER.

DISTANCES IN LAND MILES.

	London Bridge	Thames Tunnel	Deptford Cattle Mkt.	Greenwich, east of R.N.Coll.	Blackwall Pier	Woolwich Dockyard Up.Ship	Royal Arsenal	Barking Creek	Half-way House	Rainham Creek	Erith Pier	Purfleet	Greenhithe Pier	Grays Pier	Northfleet	Gravesend Town Pier	Coal House Point	Hope Point	Shell Haven	Holy Haven	Southend Pier Opposite	Nore Light-Ship	Sheerness, Garrison Point	Mouse Light-Ship
London Bridge																								
Thames Tunnel	1½																							
Deptford Foreign Cattle Market																								
Greenwich, East of R. N. College	5		1																					
Blackwall Pier	6¼	5		1¾																				
Woolwich Dockyard, Upper Ship	9	7½		4																				
Royal Arsenal	10					1																		
Barking Creek	11½	10		7½	6½		1¼																	
Half-way House	12	11½		8	8½	4		1¼																
Rainham Creek	15	13½	11	10		6			2															
Erith Pier	16½	15		11¼	10	7½	6½			1¼														
Purfleet	16½	17		16½	12	9½	8½	7			2													
Greenhithe Pier	19	20	17½	16½	15	12½	11½	10	8½		5	3												
Grays Pier	21	21½	19	18	16½		13	11½	10			4¼	1¼											
Northfleet	25½				18½	16½					8¼	6½		2¼										
Gravesend, Town Pier	26½	24½		21½	19	17½	16½			11½	9½	7½	4½	3½	1									
Coal House Point	29									12½	11¼		5¼	6½	1½	2¾								
Hope Point	32½								19½	17½	16	14	11	9¼	7½	4½	1¾							
Shell Haven	33½								20½	19	17	14	12½	10¼	8½	5½	3							
Holy Haven																	7	4	2½					
Southend Pier, Opposite	41½	43	40½							28	23	21½	18½	14½	12	9	7½							
Nore Light-Ship	48½	47		44				35½			31	27	25½	22½	18½	16	13	11½						
Sheerness, Garrison Point	52½										34	31	28½	26½	20	17	15½		4					
Mouse Light-Ship	58	54½	52	51	49½	47	46	44½	43		39¼	36½	31½	33	30½	26½	20½	22½	20	19½	11¼	7½	3½	

INDEX.

INDEX.

MAPS OF THE RIVER THAMES.

F

INDEX TO MAPS.

NAME	No of MAP	LETTER	FIGURE
Barking Creek	2	H	1
Barking, or False, Point	2	I	2
Barking Reach	2	I	2
Barking Reach	3	A	2
Battle Bridge Lower Steam Tier	1	B	2
Battle Bridge Stairs	1	B	2
Battle Bridge Upper Steam Tier	1	B	2
Beckton Pier	2	H	2
Beckton Station, G E R	2	F	1
Beckton Steam Collier Tier	2	H	2
Bell Wharf Stairs	1	E	1
Bell Wharf Tier	1	E	1
Belvedere Station, S.E.&C R	3	D	5
Benfleet Creek	7	A	2
Billingsgate Market	1	B	1
Billmeroy Creek	5	F	4
Blackheath	1	I	6
Blackheath Hill Station, S E &C R	1	H	6
"Black Prince," Watkin's Hulk, Gravesend	5	G	5
Black Shelf	4	I	3
Blackwall Lane and Causeway	2	A	4
Blackwall Pier	1	I	1
Blackwall Point	1	I	2
Blackwall Point	2	A	3
Blackwall Point Dry Dock	1	I	2
Blackwall Stairs	1	I	2
Blackwall Station	1	I	1
Blackwall Tunnel	1	I	2
Blackwall Tunnel, Northern entrance	1	H	1
Blackwall Tunnel, Southern entrance	1	I	3

INDEX TO MAPS

NAME	No of MAP	LETTER	FIGURE
Charlton Causeway	2	C	4
Charlton Junction, S E & C R	2	C	5
Charlton Lower Steam Collier Tier	2	C	4
Charlton Parish Wharf	2	B	4
Charlton Pier	2	D	4
Charlton Upper Steam Collier Tier	2	B	4
Chemical Works, Blackwall Point	2	A	4
Chemical Works Silvertown	2	C	3
Cherry Garden Pier	1	D	2
Christchurch Draw Dock	1	I	4
Church Hole Tier	1	D	2
Church Stairs	1	D	2
Cliffe	6	D	5
Cliffe Battery	6	B	5
Cliffe Canal	6	O	5
Cliffe Creek	6	B	4
Cliffe Fleet	6	E	3
Cliffe Fleet	6	E	4
Cliffe Marshes	6	C	4
Cliffe Saltings	6	B	4
Cliffe Station, S E & C R	6	D	6
Clyde Wharf	2	A	3
Coal Derrick, " Atlas " No 1, Erith	3	H	6
Coal Derrick, " Atlas " No 2	2	A	4
Coal Derrick, " Atlas " No 3	2	B	4
Coal House Battery	6	A	4
Coal House Point	6	A	5
Coal Wharf, Grays Thurrock	5	A	1
Coast Guard Watch Vessel " Drake "	6	B	4
Cocoa Nut Stairs	1	G	4

NAME	No of MAP	LETTER.	FIGURE
Cold Harbour Point	3	G	5
Commercial Dock Pier and Stairs	1	F	3
Connaught Road Station, G E R	2	C	2
Cooling	6	E	5
Cooling Marshes	6	F	4
"Cornwall" Training Ship Purfleet	4	B	2
"Countess of Erne, Steam Cutter Coal Co " Hulk Gravesend	5	G	5
Cov Fleet	6	G	4
Crayford Ness	3	I	6
Creek Bridge Deptford	1	H	5
Crescent Wharf (Chemical Works)	2	C	1
Cross Ness	3	B	2
Cubitt Town Dry Dock	1	I	4
Cubitt Town Tier	1	I	4
Cuckolds Point	1	F	2
Curtis & Harveys Powder Magazine Hulk Lower Reach	6	B	4
Curtiss Magazine, Halfway Reach	3	E	3
Custom House	1	B	1
Custom House, Lower Stairs	1	B	1
Custom House Pier, Gravesend	5	F	5
Custom House Station, G E R	2	B	2
Custom House, Upper Stairs	1	B	1
DAGENHAM	3	C	1
Dagenham Breach	3	D	1
Dagenham Marshes	3	D	1
Dagnam Saltings	6	I	4
Dartford Creek	4	A	3
Dartford Marshes	4	A	3
Deadmans or South Coast Lower Tier	1	F	3

NAME	No of MAP	LETTER	FIGURE
Erith Reach	3	F	5
Erith Station, S E &C R	3	F	6
Erith Upper Tier	3	G	5
' Exmouth" Training Ship, Grays	5	A	2
FENCHURCH Street Station	1	B	1
Folly House Tier	1	I	3
Foreign Cattle Market	1	G	4
Fountain Dry Dock	1	D	2
Fountain Hole Steam Tier	1	D	2
Fountain Stairs	1	D	2
Frindsbury Marshes	6	F	4
Fuller s Wharf	2	H	2
GALLION Point	2	G	3
Gallion Reach	2	G	2
Gallions Lower Steam Collier Tier	2	H	3
Gallions Upper Steam Collier Tier	2	H	3
Garden Stairs	1	H	5
Gas Works, Northfleet	5	B	5
Gas Works, Silvertown	2	D	3
George s Stairs	1	F	
George s Stairs Lower Steam Tier	1	C	
George's Stairs Upper Steam Tier	1	C	2
Glengall Dry Dock	1	G	3
Globe Pier	1	E	1
Globe Pond, Surrey Commercial Docks	1	E	2
Golden Anchor Stairs	1	I	4
Government Powder Magazines, Barking Reach	2	I	2
Grain Edge Buoy	7	F	6

13

NAME	No of MAP	LETTER	FIGURE
Prince Regent's Wharf (Chemical Works)	2	C	4
Prince's Dry Dock	1	E	2
Prince's Stairs	1	D	2
Prince's Stairs, Lower Tier	1	D	2
Prince's Stairs, Middle Tier	1	D	2
Prince's Stairs, Upper Tier	1	D	2
Purfleet	4	B	2
Purfleet Station, L T & S R	4	C	2
QUEBEC Pond, Surrey Commercial Docks	1	E	3
RAINHAM Creek	3	F	2
Rainham Ferry House	3	G	3
Rainham Marshes	3	G	3
Rainham Petroleum Tier	3	G	4
Rainham Station, L T & S R	3	G	1
Ratcliff Cross Stairs	1	E	1
Ratcliff Cross Tier	1	E	1
Redham Mead	6	C	4
Red Hut, East Tilbury Marshes	6	A	4
Regent Dry Dock	1	G	2
Regent's Canal Dock	1	F	1
River Medway	7	G	6
River Middle Buoy	7	D	3
River Ravensbourne	1	G	6
Roff's Pier, Woolwich	2	F	4
Rosherville	5	D	6
Rosherville Gardens	5	D	5
Rosherville Pier	5	D	5
Rosherville Station, S E & C R	5	D	6

INDEX TO MAPS

NAME.	No of MAP.	LETTER	FIGURE
St Clement or Fiddler Reach	4	H	5
Stepney Station G E R	1	F	1
St George s Stairs	1	C	2
St Katharine Docks	1	C	1
St Katharine Steam Tier	1	C	2
St Mary Marshes	6	H	4
St Mary s Bay	6	H	3
St Mary s Hoo	6	H	5
Stoke	6	I	6
Stone Marshes	4	D	5
Stone Ness	4	G	5
Stone Stairs	1	E	1
Stone Stairs Tier	1	E	1
St Saviour's Dock	1	C	2
Submarine Cable Department (Post Office Telegraphs)	2	D	4
Sugar Refinery, Silvertown'	2	D	4
" Samatra," Kelsall Bros ' Hulk, Gravesend	5	G	5
Surrey Canal Stairs	1	E	2
Surrey Canal Tier	1	E	2
Surrey Lock, Surrey Commercial Docks	1	E	2
Swanscombe Marshes	4	I	6
Swatchway	7	E	5
TANK Storage Oil Company, Purfleet	4	D	3
Tay Wharf (Jam Factory)	2	D	3
Telegraph Wharf	2	C	1
Thames & Medway Canal	6	A	6
Thames & Medway Canal, entrance and basin	5	F	5
Thames Haven Station, L.T & S R	6	D	2
Thames Iron Works	2	A	2

INDEX TO MAPS.

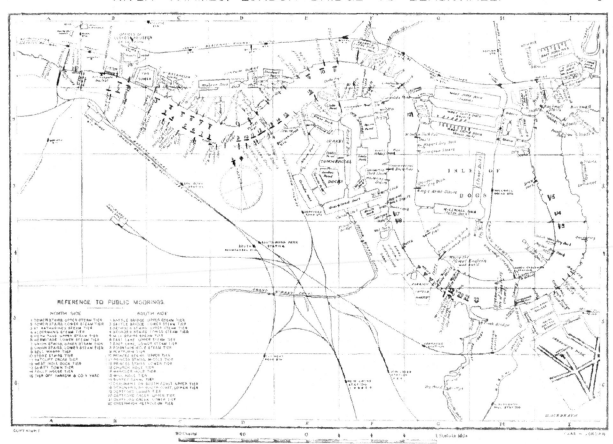

REFERENCE TO PUBLIC MOORINGS.

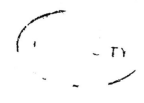

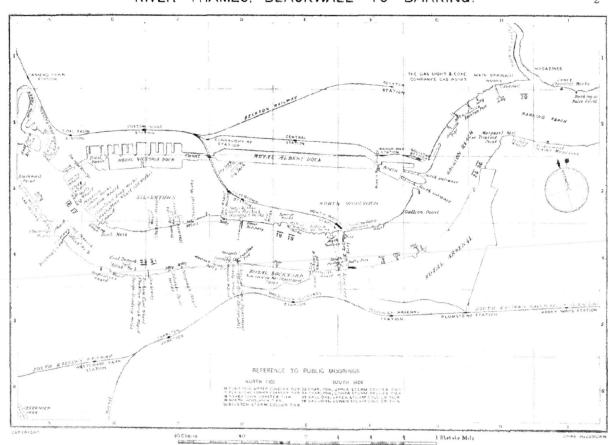

REFERENCE TO PUBLIC MOORINGS

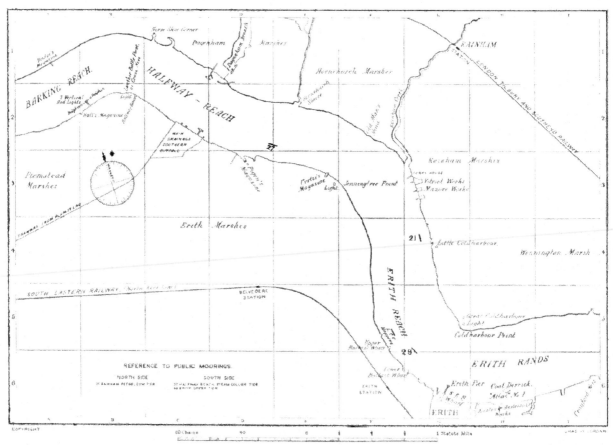

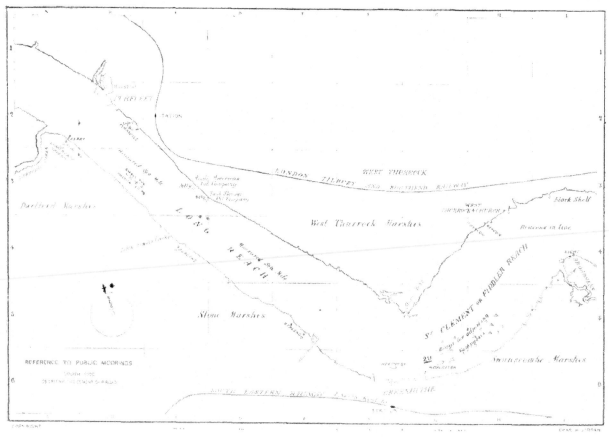

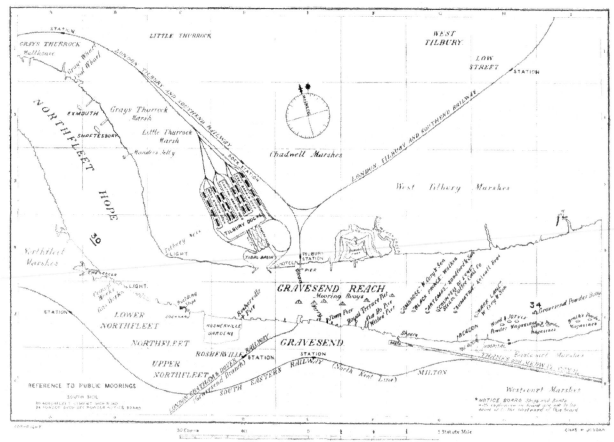

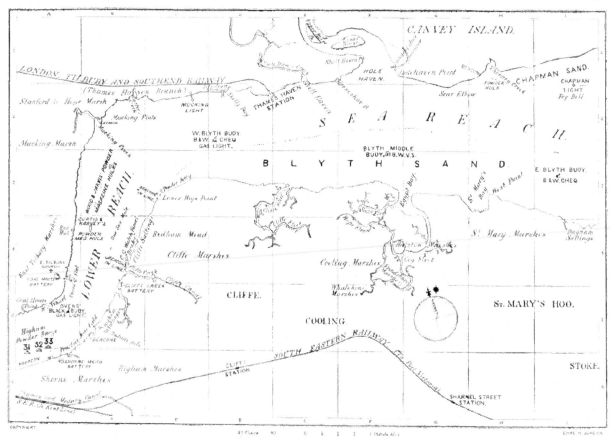

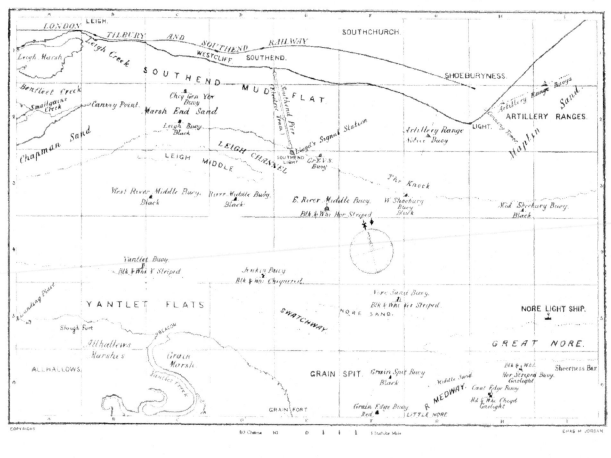

CPSIA information can be obtained at www.ICGtesting.com
Printed in the USA
BVOW09s0959210415

397042BV00012B/124/P

9 781179 894744